What people are saying about

21 Ways to Worship

(Excerpts from some of the reviews received.
Full reviews can be found at www.mercysong.com)

"*21 Ways to Worship* is a delightful, practical, and profound read — a much-needed gift for the Church! Though I have been a daily worshiper of the Blessed Sacrament for twenty-two years, I learned new ways to deepen my holy hour. This book will bless every reader in a unique and personal way. I highly recommend it."

— Kathleen Beckman
AUTHOR OF REKINDLE EUCHARISTIC AMAZEMENT
AND BEHOLD THE LAMB OF GOD
RADIO MARIA'S HOST ON "LIVING EUCHARIST"
WWW.KATHLEENBECKMAN.COM

"If you've ever struggled with making a Holy Hour, Vinny Flynn's *21 Ways to Worship* is a great resource to help you develop a deeper, more intimate relationship with our Eucharistic Lord. In simple-to-understand language, Flynn offers sage advice on how to get the most out of your time with Jesus. From journaling and surrender to visualization and the role of Mary, this short, easy read is a delight for those who, like me, need a little help in front of the Eucharist!"

— Patrick Novecosky
AWARD-WINNING CATHOLIC JOURNALIST
EDITOR-IN-CHIEF, LEGATUS MAGAZINE
WWW.PATRICK̶̶̶̶OSKY.COM

"Many adoration chapels have small libraries where reading material is made available for those who come to worship and adore Jesus in the Blessed Sacrament. Vinny Flynn's latest book *21 Ways to Worship* deserves a spot on all those sacred shelves! It offers fresh insights into how to spend time with Jesus, and will greatly increase the reader's love for our Eucharistic Lord."

— Fr. Donald Calloway, MIC
INTERNATIONALLY KNOWN SPEAKER
AUTHOR, *NO TURNING BACK: A WITNESS TO MERCY*
WWW.FATHERCALLOWAY.COM

"*21 Ways to Worship* is brilliant! An adoration chapel is the ultimate classroom of silence — there you will find peace, clarity, and the friendship of a lifetime!"

— Matthew Kelly
NEW YORK TIMES BESTSELLING AUTHOR OF *REDISCOVER CATHOLICISM*
WWW.MATTHEWKELLY.ORG

"How do we worship God? Scripture constantly reminds us to adore Him, but how? Help is on the way. *21 Ways to Worship* opens Scripture and the rich tradition of the Church to reveal the secrets to profound and meaningful worship of God. This book not only provides the why but also the how."

— Steve Ray
AUTHOR OF *CROSSING THE TIBER* AND PRODUCER OF *FOOTPRINTS OF GOD* VIDEOS
TOUR GUIDE TO BIBLICAL LANDS
WWW.CROSSINGTHETIBER.COM

21
Ways to Worship

A GUIDE TO EUCHARISTIC ADORATION

Vinny Flynn

MercySong

STOCKBRIDGE, MASSACHUSETTS
PUBLISHED BY MERCYSONG, INC.

Stockbridge, Massachusetts USA
www.mercysong.com

IN COLLABORATION WITH IGNATIUS PRESS
San Francisco, California, USA

Library of Congress Control No: 2012912931

ISBN: 978-1-884479-44-1

Design by Mary Flannery
Cover Photo by Fr. Manuel Dorantes
(taken at Saint Clement Church, Chicago, IL)

PRINTED IN CANADA
August 2012

TO THE SISTERS OF THE MONASTERY OF THE VISITATION
TYRINGHAM, MASSACHUSETTS
IN WHOSE CHAPEL THIS BOOK WAS WRITTEN

May God continue to hold you in His Heart!

"Come, then, let us bow down and worship,
bending the knee before the Lord, our maker.
For he is our God, and we are his people,
the flock he shepherds."

— PSALM 95

CONTENTS

JUST DO IT!

Anytime people start talking about Eucharistic Adoration, one question always seems to come up: "A whole hour? What'll I do for a whole hour?"

The purpose of this little book is to present at least a partial answer to that question — enough to encourage you to give it a try if you've never done it, or to offer some additional suggestions if you've already spent some time in Adoration and would like to experiment with more ways to pray while you're there.

I promise you an easy read — nothing difficult here. Just a personal sharing of some of the things that have been most fruitful for me and that have helped me develop a more meaningful relationship with God. Each chapter offers you simple, specific ideas or methods to try. If they work for you, fine. If not, hopefully they'll inspire you to come up with some new ideas of your own.

Keep in mind that none of these suggested ways to pray are things you "have" to do or even "ought" to do. There really are no "rules" for what to do during Adoration, and if I could only tell you one thing in answer to the question of how to spend your hour, I would simply say, "It doesn't matter. Just do it!" Ignore any concerns, fears, doubts, or worries about what to do for an hour. Especially ignore any of the "good reasons" you may have about why you can't really fit it into your schedule. Just make it happen, and it will change your life in ways you can't even imagine.

I'm convinced that the most important thing to understand about Adoration is that it is not only for a select group of people; it's for everyone — and it's *not optional*. To grow spiritually, you *must* adore!

Ever wonder why receiving the Eucharist is called "Communion?" The word means "union with," and that's why God gave us this great gift, so that by receiving it, we could become progressively more united with Him. Union with God is the purpose of Eucharist; indeed, the purpose of our whole earthly life. Holy Communion must become *wholly* communion: complete union with God so that we can be with Him forever. As Pope Benedict XVI writes,

> Receiving Communion means entering into communion with Jesus Christ. ... What is given us here is not a piece of a body, not a thing, but him, the Resurrected one himself — the person who shares himself with us in love. ... This means that receiving Communion is always a personal act.
>
> *GOD IS NEAR US*, P. 81

The Eucharist calls us to a personal relationship with the person of Jesus Christ, and that can't happen if all you do is receive Him in Communion once a week, or even once a day. Building a relationship with another person takes time.

Think about your other relationships. Can you have a close relationship with your parents, your spouse, your children, your friends, without spending time with them?

> "Communicating with Christ," the pope explains, "demands that we gaze on him, allow him to gaze on us, listen to him, get to know him. Adoration is simply the personal aspect of Communion. ... God is waiting for us in Jesus Christ in the Blessed Sacrament. Let us not leave him waiting in vain! Let us not, through distraction and lethargy, pass by the greatest and most important thing life offers us."
>
> *GOD IS NEAR US*, PP. 97, 102-103

So, don't worry about what you're going to do for an hour, or how you're going to do it. Just do it!

1

TAKE OFF YOUR SHOES!

After Mass one morning I had an experience that left me with a new way of beginning any time of Adoration. I had closed my eyes and was trying to focus my mind and heart to enter into Adoration using a method of contemplative prayer that I'll explain later (Chapter 15). I immediately felt blocked and sensed that I was being denied entrance into Christ's presence.

Surprised and confused, I thought to myself, "What's going on?" As if in answer to my unspoken question, I heard in my mind, "Take off your shoes!"

The words were followed by a mental image of Moses approaching the burning bush and hearing the Lord command him, "Remove the sandals from your feet, for the place where you stand is holy ground" (Exodus 3:5).

"Holy ground!" What ground could be more holy than the place where Jesus is present Body and Blood, Soul and Divinity, present alive and glorious, as He is in heaven, without leaving heaven, present together with the Father and the Holy Spirit and with the whole company of heaven? [See *7 Secrets of the Eucharist*, Chapter 2]

Yeah, I think I need to take off my shoes. I'm trying to enter heavenly realities while I'm weighted down with things of the earth.

What are the shoes?

Anything that is not of God or that might prevent you from being completely attentive to God; any of the stuff of darkness that could keep you from grasping the light. So many things, and it can be different stuff every day: unconfessed sins or left-over attachments to sin; inordinate desires and attachments; grudges, unforgiveness, hurts, resentments, bitterness, negative thoughts, attitudes, feelings, preoccupations, fears, anxieties — and on and on. Sometimes I'm not wearing shoes; I'm wearing hip boots!

How do you take off your shoes?

First, recognize what you are about to do. You are Moses standing before the burning bush. You are daring to enter the real, living, here-and-now presence of God Himself. As soon as you acknowledge that reality, you'll know what doesn't fit with it. And you can start by asking God to help:

> "Lord, help me to let go of anything that is not of You, anything of darkness, anything of sin, anything that is offensive to You, anything that could keep me from uniting myself with You."

There's no set formula for it. Use any words that come to mind, or don't use words at all, but just use your thoughts or imagine releasing everything that needs to go. Sometimes I just breathe for a while. As I breathe in, I think "Come Lord Jesus"; and as I breathe out, I think, "Set me free"; and I imagine something leaving me with each breath as the power of Christ pushes it out.

If it helps to have some prayer beginnings at hand, here are a few to get you started:

> "Lord, I repent of ..."
> "Lord, I let go of ..."
> "Lord, free me from ..."

Or, one of my favorites,

> "Mary, come in with your broom and sweep my mind and heart clean so I can enter the heart of Jesus with you."

2

Evict the Tenants!

So many images to share with you for this one! The first is from a talk I heard by Babsie Bleasdell. It's the image of a landlord — or landlady — evicting tenants.

It's a pretty harsh image, and it brought to mind another harsh image — the scene where Jesus used a whip to drive the money-changers out of the temple because they were defiling His Father's house (Jn 2:12-22).

Babsie, of course, was talking about a different temple, the living temple of the body. "Do you not know," asks St. Paul, "that you are the Temple of God, and that the Spirit of God dwells within you?" (1 Cor 3:16-17).

What defiles this temple of God that dwells within? The unwanted tenants that occupy our hearts. "Out of the heart," the Lord tells us, "come evil intentions, murder, adultery, fornication, theft, false witness, slander. These are what defile a person" (Mt 15:18).

Babsie explained that we all, at times, entertain some pretty undesirable guests in our hearts. We may not have consciously invited them, may not even know they're there; but they have taken up residence and are unwilling to leave on their own. They are defiling the temple, and we need to get rid of them — to clean house, so to speak.

How do we evict them? We choose the whip that is best-suited for the type of tenants we're dealing with. Let me give you another image that may help.

Who's on the Throne?

Christ told us that the Kingdom of God is within us (Lk 17:21). As in every kingdom, there's a king, seated on a throne. Your heart is the kingdom. Who's on the throne? If it's not Jesus Christ, you have some evicting to do. As the lyrics of an old hymn express it, "Cast all false idols from the throne. The Lord is God and He alone."

What's an idol? Anything, or anyone, that you have allowed to become more important than God. It can even be something good — your job, your appearance, your social life, sporting events, even religious activities — anything that you've become so attached or addicted to that you are neglecting your responsibilities to other people and failing to keep God at the center of your life.

How do you cast these idols from the throne? It may be that all that is needed is an extension of "taking off your shoes." Just close your eyes and imagine entering your heart. See the throne, and try to discern who or what is sitting there.

If nothing specific comes to mind, ask the Lord to help: "Lord, if there's anyone or anything that I've allowed to become so important that it's pushed You off the throne, get rid of it. Come into the temple of my heart with Your whip and drive out anything that is not of You."

The World, the Flesh, and the Devil

At other times, we may need a stronger cleansing of the temple. You may have heard that the temptations that beset us often come from the world, the flesh, or the devil — or sometimes all three.

- ■ *The World* Looking into our hearts, we may find that the throne has been occupied by secular attitudes, ideas, values, concerns, or ambitions fostered by the world around us.

- ■ *The Flesh* On a deeper level, we may discover that Christ has been pushed off the throne by needs, attachments, self-centered desires, or resentments that stem from our own human weakness — what the Church calls *concupiscence*, our inclination to sin.

■ *The Devil* Deeper still, there may be evil spirits that have found an entryway. The cartoon portrayals of a little red devil whispering in one ear and a little bright angel whispering in the other reflect a real battle raging around or within us much of the time.

And so, St. Paul exhorts us, "Put on the armor of God so that you may be able to stand firm against the tactics of the devil. For our struggle is not with flesh and blood but with the principalities, with the powers, with the world rulers of this present darkness, with the evil spirits in the heavens" (Eph 6:11-12).

Am I suggesting you might be "possessed?" No! That you need an exorcist? No! Evil spirits try to confuse us, influence us, exhaust us, and draw us away from God in all sorts of ways. In most situations, it's not a matter of a spirit taking control of you; it's more comparable to being surrounded by a swarm of nasty mosquitoes that irritate and distract you so that you just can't function as well.

We'll come back to how to get rid of the "mosquitoes," but first let's look at some examples of how "the world, the flesh, and the devil" often work together to occupy our hearts in a way that can gradually draw us away from God and even cripple us spiritually.

■ A 20 year-old college student, through books, the news media, movies, teachers, and discussions with friends, is exposed to secular ideas and anti-religious attitudes (*The World*). His prayer life begins to suffer, he stops going to Mass, and he begins questioning the authority of his parents and the teachings of the Church (*The Flesh*). Finding an entryway, spirits of confusion, self-centeredness, and rebellion enter his heart (*The Devil*). He's frustrated and unhappy, but doesn't know why.

■ A young girl, growing up in a family environment of violence and rejection, experiences constant criticism, neglect, and physical abuse (*The World*). Feeling somehow to blame, she withdraws into herself, vowing that she will never be like them and never allow herself to be hurt again (*The Flesh*). Finding an entryway, spirits of insecurity, abandonment, and unforgiveness enter her heart (*The Devil*). She's feels isolated and unable to find meaningful relationships with others.

■ A middle-aged, married man is exposed to sex-based TV, computer, and magazine ads and explicit sex scenes in movies and novels (*The World*). He finds himself giving in to impure thoughts and sexual fantasies and begins looking at pornography on his computer (*The Flesh*). Finding an entryway, spirits of lust, addiction, and despair come into his heart (*The Devil*). He wants to be free of this, but feels completely helpless.

13

A few years ago, I was given a really helpful book that makes it easy to recognize the kinds of entryways that spirits use to influence us. It's called *Unbound: A Practical Guide to Deliverance*, and it's written by Neal Lozano, a great Catholic teacher and writer.

Lozano shows how sneaky these uninvited guests can be, waiting for a door to open even a little so they can stick a foot in and get a toehold on our lives. And he provides very practical ways that we can get rid of these "mosquitoes" by identifying the doors we have opened and learning how to close them. It's well worth reading.

Another writer and spiritual director, Fr. George Kosicki, CSB, also teaches about the devious tactics of evil spirits, and he has a favorite "whip" or "battle technique" for getting rid of them. He calls it "Squashing the Bug."

He explains that Satan and his cohorts know our weak points, so they use the same old "knapsack of tricks" over and over again to get us to yield to anger or fear or jealousy or self-pity or impurity, etc., etc. We need to first identify the trick being used and then turn to Mary.

"She is the one," Fr. Kosicki says, "who crushes the head of the serpent with the heel of her offspring. As the heel, the humblest, lowest part of the Body of Christ, we, the children of Mary, experience the bite of Satan. But we can turn to our Mother to show us how to crush the head of Satan" (See Gen 3:15 and Rev 12:17).

"How do we do it?" he asks. "With a laugh. With the joy of the victory that has been given to the Woman. We can turn to Mary with a laugh and say: 'Mary, look at the old boy. He's using the same old trick of anger. Step on his head, Mary. *Squash the bug!* Crush that serpent with your heel. The victory is yours, Mary, and is given to us, your offspring. *Squash the bug!*'"

Another "whip" that Fr. Kosicki recommends is the daily practice of taking authority over evil spirits in the name of Jesus — a kind of spiritual maintenance. I've adapted his authority prayer and included it here as a sample for you. You don't have to use this exact wording, but can modify it in whatever way works for you. The only necessary ingredient is to take authority in the name of Jesus by the power of His Precious Blood.

Authority Prayer

By Fr. George Kosicki and Vinny Flynn

In the name of the Father and of the Son and of the Holy Spirit. Amen.

Thank You, Jesus for Your Eucharistic presence here and throughout the world. Thank You for Your passion, death, and resurrection, and Your victory over sin, death, and Satan. Thank You for giving the victory to Mary and, through her, to us.

In the name of Jesus Christ and by the power of His Precious Blood, I take authority over you, Satan, and all you other evil spirits in or around me or _____. [*List names of family members, friends, or others who come to mind.*]

I set the Blood of Jesus upon you, especially you spirits of _____. [*List whatever spirits come to mind*], and I order you to be gone, bound to Jesus, never more to interfere with our lives.

Lord, Jesus, we belong to You. Fill us with Your Holy Spirit. Fill us with Your mercy. Send Your angels to guard and guide, comfort and instruct us, so that we may love and serve You every moment of our lives.

[*Say the "Our Father" and conclude with, "For the kingdom and the power and the glory are Yours, now and always and forever. Amen."*]

EVICT THE TENANTS!

3

RUN TO DADDY!

Our presence before the Blessed Sacrament is a witness to our belief that what looks like a wafer of bread in the monstrance is actually the real, full presence of Jesus, and we are there to adore Him. But our adoration of Jesus — our focus on Him — has to lead us to the Father. It has to reveal to us who the Father is.

St. Paul tells us that Jesus is the visible "image of the invisible God" (Col 1:15). Who's the invisible God? The Father. During His Last Supper discourse, Jesus told the apostles that He was going to His Father's house to prepare a place for them, and He made it clear that through Him and Him alone, we have access to the Father:

> I am the way, the truth, and the life. No one comes to the Father except through me. If you know me, you will know my Father also.
>
> JN 14:6-7

The more we get to know Jesus, the more we will come to know the Father. And the key to getting to know Jesus is Adoration. The hours we spend in Adoration enable us to really meet Him, to come to know Him, person to person, to unite ourselves to Him so completely that, through Him, we meet the Father. As Pope John Paul II explains :

> When we contemplate him in the Blessed Sacrament of the Altar, Christ draws near to us and becomes more intimate to us than we are to ourselves. He grants us a share in his divine life in a transforming union and, in the Spirit, he gives us access to the Father.
>
> FEAST OF CORPUS CHRISTI, MAY 28, 1996

When Philip asked Jesus, "Lord, show us the Father," Jesus responded:

> Have I been with you all this time, Philip, and you still don't know me? Whoever has seen me has seen the Father.
>
> JN 14:8-9

It was not an isolated remark, not a new teaching. He was

constantly praying to the Father, talking about the Father, trying to help them "see" the Father.

> The Father and I are one. I came down from heaven not to do my own will but the will of the one who sent me. ... The one who sent me is with me. He has not left me alone, because I always do what is pleasing to Him.
>
> JN 10:30; 6:38; 8:29

We have to recognize what Pope John Paul II said repeatedly throughout his encyclical *Rich in Mercy*: Jesus came to show us that God is a "Father who is rich in mercy," a Father who just wants to love us, to bless us, to bestow Himself upon us. Even the cross, the pope continued, "speaks and never ceases to speak of God the Father, who is absolutely faithful to His eternal love. ... Believing in the crucified Son means seeing the Father" (*Rich in Mercy* #7).

The next time you attend Mass, notice the constant references to the Father throughout all the prayers. It's all about the Father! In every celebration of the Mass we are joining Christ's eternal offering of Himself to the Father in atonement for the sins of the world.

One of the most appropriate prayers to say during adoration is the Chaplet of Divine Mercy, because it's like an extension of the Mass:

> Eternal Father, I offer you the Body and Blood, Soul and Divinity of Your dearly beloved Son, Our Lord Jesus Christ, in atonement for our sins and those of the whole world.
>
> *DIARY*, 476

The offering we make through this prayer reflects the Council of Trent definition of the Eucharist: "the Body and Blood, together with the Soul and Divinity of our Lord Jesus Christ" (*Catechism*, #1374). We're offering the Eucharist to the Father! What better way to start adoration than that?

The day after Jesus revealed the prayers of the Chaplet to St. Faustina, He told her: **"Every time you enter the chapel, immediately recite the prayer which I taught you yesterday"** (*Diary*, 476).

Everything comes from and must lead back to the Father. When we come to Eucharistic Adoration, we are running to the embrace of our Father. In *Rich in Mercy*, Pope John Paul II said,

> Our Father ... is always waiting for us to have recourse to Him in every need and always waiting for us to study His mystery: the mystery of the Father and His love.
>
> #2

So when we come before Jesus in Eucharistic Adoration, He is not alone. He is never alone. With Him — always — is the

Father, the Holy Spirit, and all of heaven. (For more on this, see my book *7 Secrets of the Eucharist.*)

United with our Eucharistic Lord, we bow to the Father, we talk to the Father, we pray to the Father, we ask Him to help us be His children. Below is a prayer I often use in Adoration:

> Lord Jesus, You are Mercy-made-flesh, the visible "image of the invisible God" (Col 1:15). You are the Father's love made present for us. As I gaze upon You, I see the Father, "rich in mercy," raising His hand over me in blessing, and pouring into me, through Your pierced Heart, the very life of the Trinity.
>
> Immersing myself in the living stream of blood and water that flows endlessly from Your Heart as a fountain of mercy for us, I receive the Father's blessing and recognize who I am as a child of His love.
>
> In You, Lord Jesus, I see the reflection of my own unique value and dignity as a son (daughter) of the Father, created in His image and likeness and called to be holy as He is holy. In You and with You, I will forever call God my Father and forever rejoice in the awesome reality that He loves me even as He loves you (Jn 17:23).

FROM "FATHER GOD" © 2010 VINNY FLYNN

4

KEEP IT PERSONAL!

One of the biggest mistakes, I think, that many of us make as Christians, as Catholics, is that we get used to being very formal. We have some wonderful, ritual prayers that are beautiful and can be very meaningful, but this can cause us to get used to a certain formality that can carry over into our adoration time and make it hard for us to develop a deep, personal relationship with God.

Again, as Pope Benedict says, the Eucharist "is not a piece of a body, not a thing." It's a person — a person who loves us more than we can imagine.

It's not a new problem. St. Faustina got in a lot of trouble with some of the other sisters in her congregation because she was so intimate with God, and they felt that this was not proper, not reverent. Who did she think she was to talk to God in such an informal way? But she knew that that's what God wanted. He was her Father. He wanted a relationship with her, like any good father wants with his children. He wanted to love her, to bless her. He wanted her to "have recourse to Him in every need."

We don't need to be formal with God here. He doesn't want us to be. We need to be real with Him!

In whatever you say, do, look at, or read during adoration, keep it personal, realizing that this is between you and God — and God is three persons, each of whom want a personal relationship with you.

How do you get closer to your spouse, to your children, to your friends? You have to spend time with them; you have to get to know them. A relationship takes time, and it takes personal involvement, personal commitment.

That's what Eucharistic Adoration is all about. You're there to keep Christ company, to console Him, to get to know Him, to get to know the Father, to get to know the Holy Spirit, to build a relationship, person-to-person, you and God alone.

You are getting to *know* this God, to know who He is, and then you start to realize who you are and who *you* are called *to be*. This is the God who didn't just create you. He fathered you into existence, chose you from all the millions of persons who could have come from the union of your father and mother.

He chose you! He promised to love you forever. He carved you in the palm of His hand. This is the person who has loved you with an everlasting love. So be personal with Him. Be real! Talk to Him!

One of the things I find helpful in this regard is to personalize scripture. Don't be afraid of scripture, and don't be afraid to make it your own. Scripture is the living word of God. It's appropriate for when — and to whom — it was written, and it has an infinite number of levels of meaning. But God can also talk to you, personally, right now, through scripture; and you can talk to Him through scripture, too.

I'm not talking about *interpretation* of scripture. I follow the Holy Spirit's direction through the Church for that. My concern here is not what a scripture passage *means*. The kind of prayers and passages I'm talking about are pretty clear in their meaning anyway. My focus here is on *responding* to the passage in such a way that it brings me into more direct and personal contact with God.

So, for example, look at this Antiphon from the *Liturgy of the Hours*:

> Come, let us give thanks to the Lord, for His great love is without end.

This is a passage *about* God and an *exhortation to thank Him* for His great, everlasting love. Its meaning is very clear, no interpretation needed. If I'm simply reading scripture, it's beautiful and inspiring just the way it is.

But I don't want to merely *read* it; I want to *fulfill* it in my life right now by obediently responding to it. So I look at the passage, acknowledge it in my mind, and then fulfill it in my now moment by my response:

> I give You thanks, oh Lord, for Your great love is
> without end.

In the same way, "Let us approach him with praise and thanksgiving" (Psalm 95) is fulfilled through a personal, obedient response: "Lord, I come before You with praise and thanksgiving."

We can even respond this way, interiorly, during Mass. Every morning at Mass, for example, when I hear the priest say, "Let us give thanks to the Lord our God," I respond with the congregation, "It is right and just." But then I immediately pray silently, "Yes, Lord, it is right and just to give You thanks and praise, so I thank You and praise You right now."

When you personalize scripture, it has such power! I wish I could give a workshop to music ministers and songwriters and discuss with them the difference between songs that are written and sung *about* God — or about *us* — and songs that are written and sung *to* God.

So many of our hymns seem so self-focused or so "informational," that they don't really lead us into prayer. Some of these songs are very beautiful and can be inspirational, but it's so much more powerful when we can sing songs in which we are directly, personally talking to God, not talking about ourselves or talking to ourselves about Him!

There are many passages from scripture that can be adapted to make them into personal communications between you and God. The psalms are an especially rich source of personalized prayer. Some of them are already personal; some are not personal at all, and some are half and half. But you can make them your own.

I've done two for you here as samples to get you started. I've included the originals and the adaptations so you can easily see the process. Psalm 100 is an example of a psalm that is not personal at all in its original form (it talks to the reader *about* God, not *to* God). Psalm 23 is an example of a half and half psalm: some of it talks *about* God; some of it talks *to* Him. The personalized version is from the lyrics I wrote for the title song of my *Endless Mercy* CD.

The originals are beautiful, but the little wording changes allow you to make them your own, and it becomes very powerful personal prayer. You're talking to God now; you're not just reciting scripture.

When you personalize scripture, you are personally responding to God's Word, taking it into yourself, your life, your situation. You are making a decision to mean what you're saying, because now you're talking directly to God and saying some really personal things.

Psalm 100 (Original)

Cry out with joy to the Lord,
all the earth.
Serve the Lord with gladness.
Come before him,
singing for joy.

Know that he, the Lord, is God.
He made us, we belong to him,
we are his people,
the sheep of his flock.

Go within his gates,
giving thanks.
Enter his courts with songs
of praise.
Give thanks to him
and bless his name.

Indeed, how good is the Lord,
eternal his merciful love.
He is faithful from age to age.

Psalm 100 (Personalized)

With all the earth I cry out
with joy to you, oh Lord.
I will serve you with gladness.
I will come before you,
singing for joy.

For you, oh Lord, are God.
You made us, we belong to you,
we are your people,
the sheep of your flock.
So I come within your gates,
giving thanks.

I enter your courts
with songs of praise,
giving thanks to you
and blessing your name.

How good you are, oh Lord!
How eternal your merciful love!
You are faithful from age to age.

Psalm 23 *(Original)*

The Lord is my shepherd;
there is nothing I shall want.
Fresh and green are the pastures
where he gives me repose.
Near restful waters he leads me,
to revive my drooping spirit.
He guides me along
the right path;
He is true to his name.

If I should walk in the
valley of darkness
no evil would I fear.
You are there with your crook
and your staff;
with these you give me comfort.

You have prepared a banquet
for me in the sight of my foes.
My head you have anointed
with oil;
my cup is overflowing.
Surely goodness and kindness
shall follow me
all the days of my life.
In the Lord's own house shall
I dwell forever and ever.

Psalm 23 *(Personalized)*

O Lord, you are my shepherd,
You fill my life with all
I'll ever need.
You lead me beside
the still waters,
You restore my soul.
You lead me beside
the still waters,
Your endless mercy restores
my soul.

Though I must walk
in the darkness of the valley,
I fear no evil with you
by my side.
Your rod and staff give me
comfort and courage to walk
In the right paths with you
as my guide.

You spread a table before me
in the presence of my foes,
And you anoint me
with your Spirit from above.
Your endless mercy
will follow me
through all of my days
And keep me in the
kingdom of your love.

From *Endless Mercy* © 1999 Vinny Flynn

5

Do it Write!

Pardon the pun; I couldn't resist. This is about journaling, and there are all kinds of ways to journal. My feeling is that whatever way you use is all write (Oops, sorry; there I go again). But seriously, don't be afraid to try this. There is no "right" way, no "correct" method. Experiment with it until you find a way, or various ways that work for you. (Just remember the "rule" about keeping everything personal.)

Just bring a notebook, or a style of journal that you like, into the chapel with you and start writing in it. You can record your thoughts, feelings, experiences, problems, questions, insights you get from praying or reading, quotes you come across and want to remember, etc.

And, for real spiritual growth, you can actually dare to write to God. You can talk to Him, one-on-one in writing. Talk to Him about anything:

> "Wow, what a terrible day this has been, God. I'm trying to trust that You've allowed it for some reason, and that You can turn it to good, so I thank You for it anyway, but it's really hard."

Don't be fake with God, don't be formal, don't be polite, don't pretend to feel things you don't feel, don't say the things you think He wants to hear. Don't try to impress Him. Don't try to earn His approval. He knows everything about you, and He loves you anyway. Remember that you're talking to a person, not a concept. This is the one person in your life with whom you can be completely open, completely honest, completely real. Be who you are with Him!

I want to share with you what I think are the two most fruitful ways to begin writing in your journal when you first enter into Adoration. Let's start with the "runner up," my suggestion #2:

Identify where you are. Acknowledge Christ's presence, say whatever initial prayer you want to say, open your journal, and tune into your body. What's going on with you right now? What are you aware of in yourself at this moment, physically, mentally, emotionally, spiritually? Tune in to it, and then share it with God. He knows anyway, of course, but talking about it with Him will make it clearer to you and will give Him permission to respond — with a thought, an insight, a feeling, an outpouring of grace.

As you write, if a prayer that relates to what you're saying occurs to you, write that, too:

> "Lord, I'm so exhausted right now ... stayed up too late last night ... that was dumb! ... especially since I was already so nervous about my interview today. I give it to You, Lord. Refresh me, keep me alert, and help me to relax and trust in You."

Now for the winner! My #1 suggestion for how to start your journal entries — and your day:

Thank Him! Open your journal, and with your mind focused on the reality that Jesus is right here with you, in person, write, "Thank You, Jesus, for ..." or "Thank You, Jesus, that ..." Finish the statement by listing at least five things, events, people, situations, or whatever, that you are grateful for.

Sometimes when I open my journal, I'm not conscious of feeling grateful for anything. I've been too depressed, or overwhelmed or distracted or preoccupied — or just too busy taking the good things for granted and whining about everything else. But as soon as I write the words, "Thank You, Jesus," things come to mind, and I start to realize how much I have to be thankful for. Usually I can't stop after the first five things, and the pages fill up quickly as the awareness of one blessing leads to another.

The best advice my spiritual director ever gave me — and tried to hammer into my head — is to practice the spirituality of St. Paul:

> Dedicate yourself to thanksgiving. ... Rejoice in the Lord always, pray constantly, and in all things give thanks.
>
> COL. 3:17; 1 THES. 5:16-18

Thanking God is the antidote to depression, self-pity, anxiety, pessimism — and just about everything else that prevents us from living in the joy God wants to fill us with.

So if nothing else, use your journal to thank God. After that, use it any way that works for you. You can use it mostly as a spiritual journal to record thoughts, prayers, insights, etc. Or it can be more like a diary that you're writing in the presence of the Lord, recording things that happened during the day, things you did, things you saw, people you met.

Just be conscious as you're writing that it's not a "Dear Diary" kind of thing. Diaries don't listen; diaries don't respond. You're not just recording things, not just talking to yourself or to your diary. You're talking to God about what's going on, sharing highlights of the good things, the bad things, your doubts, fears, concerns. You're inviting God into your life, confiding in Him, putting Him in charge of everything. And He will listen and respond.

His response rarely comes through direct communication; it's more often through a thought, a feeling, an insight, an awareness, an event. But there are ways you can receive a more direct response simply by occasionally including a Q&A in your journal. You ask God questions (in writing), and then write down His answers. It's a little more daring.

When my spiritual director told me to start doing that, I said, "Yeah, right! How do I know that what I'm writing down is really something God's saying? So far, He's never tapped me on the shoulder and said, 'Vinny, I want you to build an ark.' So how do I know it's Him talking?"

His response surprised me: "It's none of your business! Don't worry about it. If it's not from God, it's just going to fall to the ground as something you've written. No harm done. If you ask Him a question, and something pops into your head, write it down and then try to respond to it."

"Lord, what can I do to please You, today?"
"Rest in My heart."

Okay, I can do that. I don't know whether that thought really came from God or just from me, but does it really matter? He's not telling me to rob a bank. If that kind of thought came to me, I'd know it wasn't from God. But is it really going to hurt me to take these words as a meditation for my day? To stay focused on God today and try to rest in His heart as I go about my work?

One variation of the Q&A that can be very fruitful is to specifically ask for a word to meditate on:

> "Lord, do You have a word for me today?"
> "Patience."
> "Ouch! Okay, I guess I needed that. I'll give it a try, Lord, but I'm going to need Your help. You know this isn't one of my strong suits."

It takes a while to get used to writing down these kinds of conversations with God without feeling completely foolish and self-conscious, but it's worth the effort. You're giving God permission to help you, to instruct you, to lead you, to comfort you. And you're building your relationship with Him, growing in your awareness that He's a real person, that He really does love you, and that He wants to be involved in your life.

And just remember, you don't have to do it right. Just do it. (I'll skip the pun this time — you get the idea.)

DO IT WRITE!

6

PICTURE THIS!

You could also call this chapter "Slideshow." You're sitting in front of the Blessed Sacrament. You may already have tried to "take off your shoes," but you realize that you're not empty yet. Our minds tend to keep going all the time, and as soon as you get rid of one thought, up pops another. So, instead of worrying about all the distractions and trying to resist them, let them come. Let it become like a slideshow.

I remember years ago when people would show their pictures on a screen with a slide projector. You'd pack a bunch of slide photos in the projector and click the remote controller every time you wanted to change slides. Now, in the digital age, people put their photos into iPhoto and click on slide show and you can set it so that the slides change automatically or manually, so it's pretty much the same process.

So, as each slide comes — a thought, a worry about your daughter, a memory of a past hurt, a concern about an upcoming meeting, a financial problem — don't try to resist it, don't dwell on it. Just acknowledge it, "look" at it in your mind for a moment, and then give it to God and let it go.

It's like, "Okay Lord, you take care of this. Next slide please." Let them come, and let them go. Usually they come fast and furious for a while, and then they slow down, and your mind gradually becomes empty and peaceful, and now you can be more attentive to God.

You can also create specific slide shows in your mind. I sometimes use slideshow prayer as a way of bringing each member of my family into the Eucharistic heart of Jesus. I just let each one sit in my mind for a moment while I pray, asking the Lord to hold him or her in his heart. Then I let that slide go and let the next one come in.

Words are optional. If it helps to pray in word thoughts, that's okay, but keep them short so that you don't stall the process. Here's some examples of the kind of short prayers you can use if you wish:

> "I give it to You, Lord."
> "Bless him, Lord."
> "Jesus, I trust in You."

"Let Your will be done, Lord."
"Let Your intentions be fulfilled."
"Mercy, Lord."

7

SAY CHEESE!

Several years ago I happened upon a method of praying that has become a daily practice for me, especially in Adoration. It's similar to the slideshow type of prayer, but more visual. It began with the Divine Mercy image, the now well-known picture of Christ with red and pale rays streaming from His Heart.

I had become accustomed to praying before the large image of the Divine Mercy that hung in my office, imagining myself in the midst of those rays as I intoned the familiar prayer, "Oh Blood and Water, which gushed forth from the Heart of Jesus as a fount of mercy for us, I trust in You" (*Diary*, 84).

On this particular day I was praying for a family member, and I found myself mentally placing him in the rays, asking the Lord to let him stay there all day to be soaked and saturated with grace in this outpouring of God's mercy. Looking for a way to remember this intention throughout the day, I dug up a photo of him and stuck it in the corner of the frame so that it was right below the rays — a visual reminder that would prompt me to renew my prayer each time I looked up and noticed it.

It made my prayer seem so much more real that I soon purchased a much larger, unframed image. I glued it to a thick piece of cardboard and, within a few weeks, there were pictures tacked all over it: my wife and children, other family members, the Pope, special friends, anyone I wanted to remember to pray for.

A variation of this photo prayer soon emerged. My wife and I decided to assign a specific day of the week to pray in a special way for each of our children (very easy to do since there are seven of them). So we gathered photos of each and set up a little "prayer table" on which we could display a different photo each day. This became especially powerful during Lent, as it prompted me to also give up something specific for each child on his or her prayer day.

But as meaningful as these two types of prayer were, the next variation proved to be the most fruitful for me, and has become a permanent part of my daily prayer life.

Years earlier I had learned that praying the *Liturgy of the Hours* (the 4-volume set of prayers known also as the Divine Office or the Breviary) is not reserved exclusively for priests and religious, but can be a fruitful practice of daily prayer for laity as well. I especially love to "pray the Office" in front of the Blessed Sacrament during Eucharistic Adoration (more about this later).

One day, concerned about a friend who was in need of prayer, I found a photo of her and put it in my breviary so I would remember to pray for her the next morning at Adoration. It was the first of many photos that I now keep in my breviary. (It doesn't have to be a breviary; any prayer book or prayer journal would serve the purpose just as well.)

How do I pray using the photos? I just look at them. "Prayer," wrote St. Therese, "is a surge of the heart." I just look at the pictures, one by one, and let my heart surge to God for each person. A photo captures much of the essence of a person. As I gaze at each photo, the person it represents becomes present to me, complete with personality traits, strengths, weaknesses, memories, conversations, needs, etc.

Sometimes actual words of prayer come to mind and are offered; sometimes there are no words. Essentially, I am simply lifting each person up to God in whatever way and for whatever period of time seems called for. It varies from day to day.

Sometimes a brief glance and momentary entrustment of the

person to God is sufficient. At other times, the same photo may bring a flood of thoughts and a longer period of prayer. I just let it happen, trusting that the Holy Spirit is directing it all.

I am now in the habit of carrying a small digital camera with me when I travel; and when someone asks for prayer, I say, "Sure! Say 'cheese.'"

SAY CHEESE!

8

PLEASE DON'T SNORE!

A lot of people are afraid that they're going to fall asleep during Adoration. And a lot of people do fall asleep. So, if you think you might fall asleep, don't go to Adoration — no, I'm only kidding! It's okay to fall asleep!

We need to remember who God is! He's a Father! A different kind of father than any of us can be. He's a perfect Father who loves you unconditionally, who is always loving you. If one of my kids comes to me (even in my weak, imperfect way of being a father) and says, "Dad, I'm really tired, and I may fall asleep, but I'd just like to be with you for a while, so can I sit in here?" — what would I say to that?

"No way, kid! If you're going to be in here with me, you need to stay awake."

Of course not! What father would do that? I would be delighted! My son or daughter wants to be with me. How awesome!

The same thing is true of work. I work in front of the Blessed Sacrament all the time. I have work that I have to do, but I'd like to be with Him. I'd like Him to bless my work. I'd like to pause now and then and talk to Him about my work.

Again, how would I feel if one of my kids comes to me and says, "I have a lot of work to do, Dad, but I don't want to be in my room. I just want to be with you. Can I sit next to you and do my work? I don't mean to be ignoring you, but I just want to be close to you." — That's every parent's dream!

God is a Father! Fall asleep in His arms!

Now, if you're in adoration with other people, and you think it's likely that you're going to fall asleep, and you know you snore (or at least breathe really heavily), then it might be good to give them permission to wake you. You can simply whisper something like, "You know, I'm liable to fall asleep, so if I do, don't be afraid to nudge me and wake me up, because I don't want to distract anyone from prayer."

Just be human. Be who you are. Be human with God; be human with the other people in Adoration.

If you find yourself falling asleep every time you go to

Adoration, you might want to pick a different hour, so that for at least some of the time, you can be alert and consciously present to the One who is present for you.

9

BEHOLD YOUR MOTHER!

I don't know why, but some people are still afraid to think
about Mary in front of the Blessed Sacrament, as if devotion
to Mary is somehow inappropriate during Eucharistic Adoration. There have even been some priests who have discouraged
devotion to Our Lady, especially during Adoration, feeling that
it takes the focus off the Eucharistic presence of Jesus.

How absurd! As if Mary would ever distract us from Jesus!
Her whole being "magnifies the Lord" (Lk 1:46)! She leads us
to Jesus, *not away* from Him. Fortunately, virtually all the popes,
saints, and mystics have taught us the truth about Mary — and
about how close she is to the Eucharist.

Pope John Paul II, in His encyclical on the Eucharist, devoted the whole final chapter to Mary under the title, "At the School of Mary: Woman of the Eucharist." He writes,

> If the Church and the Eucharist are inseparably united, the same can be said of Mary and the Eucharist.
>
> THE CHURCH OF THE EUCHARIST, #57

In his introduction to that encyclical, he explained that he was writing it to "rekindle Eucharistic amazement," and to that end he identified "the programme" that he was setting before the Church for the third millennium: "to contemplate the face of Christ, and to contemplate it with Mary." And he emphasized that this contemplation with Mary should involve recognizing Christ "*above all* in the living sacrament of his body and his blood" (#6).

The Church teaches that the Eucharist is the Body and Blood, Soul and Divinity of Jesus. At the Annunciation, through Mary's *Fiat*, the Second Person of the Trinity took on a human nature from her flesh, and in that instant ("the fullness of time") the God-Man, Jesus, became present "Body and Blood, Soul and Divinity" within her — and *only* in her. The shepherds and the wise men, and the rest of us would have to wait a while. But Mary received an extended communion.

As Pope John Paul II and Pope Benedict XVI both explain, the Annunciation was Mary's "first Holy Communion." *She was the first one asked to believe that God Himself wanted to take flesh in her, and by her Fiat she became the first living tabernacle.* In her, God had finally found a worthy temple for His presence.

Scripture records that Mary's first act after receiving the full presence of Jesus was to take Him to her cousin Elizabeth. Both popes call her Visitation to Elizabeth the "first Eucharistic procession in history," and explain that Mary was a "living monstrance." She was *transparent* to God, so united with Him that His divine presence within her *radiated* from every part of her being — so much so that the mere sound of her voice had an amazing, transforming effect upon Elizabeth and, in a sense, "baptized" John the Baptist in his mother's womb:

> When Elizabeth heard Mary's greeting, the infant leaped in her womb, and Elizabeth, filled with the Holy Spirit, cried out in a loud voice and said, "Most blessed are you among women, and blessed is the fruit of your womb."
>
> Lk 1:41-42

So, what better person than Mary to help prepare us to adore Jesus in the Blessed Sacrament, to help us become so transformed by Him that we, too, radiate His presence?

In his teachings about how we all need to "sit in the school of Mary" to learn from her about the Eucharist, Pope John Paul II explains that there is "a profound analogy" between Mary's *Fiat* and the Amen we say when we receive the Eucharist. He urges us to follow her example and let our Amen be a *Fiat*.

What an amazing insight! When I read this, it touched me so deeply that I put it into a prayer that I call the *Fiat-Amen* prayer. It's a perfect prayer to say right after receiving Communion or anytime during Adoration:

Fiat-Amen

Amen. Yes, Lord, I believe that You are truly present here, Body and Blood, Soul and Divinity, hidden under what still looks like bread. Yes, Lord, I believe that You actually want to live in me, flesh of my flesh.

Fiat, Lord. Let it be done to me according to Your will. Live in me. Let Your whole 'mode of being' pass into me — Your thoughts, Your feelings, Your attitudes, Your values, Your way of seeing and living and loving. Keep me conscious of Your presence within me as I leave this church, and let me bring You with me into the world.

Let me become living Eucharist, a living tabernacle of Your love. Let me be, like Mary, a living monstrance, bringing Your love and the power of Your Spirit to all I meet so that they, like the babe in Elizabeth's womb, may leap for joy at the tenderness of Your touch.

© 2005 VINNY FLYNN

Our Lady is inseparable from the Eucharist. She is always at the side of Jesus in the Eucharist. As you gaze at the monstrance and, with the eyes of faith, see beyond what still looks like bread and "behold the Lamb of God," you can also, in a different but very real way, "behold" your Mother with Him. (I explain this completely in *7 Secrets of the Eucharist*, so I won't repeat all of that here. But it's important to understand what the Church teaches about this.)

Only Jesus is present *sacramentally* (meaning "under the appearance of bread and wine.") But present *with* Him — always — are the Father, the Holy Spirit, Our Lady, and all of heaven.

As we pray before the monstrance, we are invited to let the trappings of earth slip away for a time as we enter into heavenly realities. We are in the presence of the Trinity; and we behold Mary, standing by her Son, encouraging us to join her and all the saints and angels as they adore Him, singing, "Holy, Holy, Holy, Lord God of Hosts."

As Pope Benedict XVI tells us:

> Mary dwells not just in the past or in the lofty spheres of heaven. ... She is and remains present and real in this historical moment; she is a person acting here and now. ... Mary comes to us as a mother, always open to the needs of her children. Through the light which streams from her face, God's mercy is made

manifest. Let us allow ourselves to be touched by her gaze, which tells us that we are loved by God and never abandoned by him.

MARY'S YES TO MAN, LOURDES HOMILY, 9/14/08

So, don't be afraid to sit in front of the Blessed Sacrament and talk to Our Lady. She's there, right next to Jesus, completely united with Him, and ready to help bring you closer to Him. And don't be afraid to pray the rosary during Adoration. As Pope John Paul II explains, the rosary is "a gospel prayer," in which we are "remembering with Mary," remembering the great events of our salvation and learning more about Jesus from Mary.

Below are two additional prayers that you may find helpful as you "behold your Mother" during Adoration:

Mary, Mother of the Lord, show us what it means to enter into communion with Christ. You offered your own flesh, your own blood to Jesus and became a living tabernacle, allowing yourself to be penetrated in body and spirit by His presence. I ask you, Holy Mother, to help me allow myself to be penetrated by that same presence, so that I may follow Him faithfully, day after day, along whatever paths He leads me.

© 2005 VINNY FLYNN
ADAPTED FROM POPE BENEDICT XVI,
CORPUS CHRISTI HOMILY, MAY, 2005

Mary, as I kneel here in the presence of your Son Jesus, I turn to you to help me adore Him more completely. Wherever Jesus is, you are with Him. It is thanks to your *Fiat*, your offering of your own body in sheer abandonment to God, that the Word became flesh in your womb.

This was the first reception of Holy Communion, and when you gave birth to the Son of God, you were the first to adore His presence among us. Throughout your life you remained in communion with your Son, always united with Him in unselfish love.

Teach me, Mary, how to adore Him as you do, how to remain always in His presence, in complete union with His holy will.

10

FOR GOD'S SAKE, SHUT UP!

The other title I had in mind for this chapter was "Please Hold the Popcorn!" I've had more than one priest tell me that hearing some people's confessions is "like being stoned to death with popcorn" — with things that don't really matter, with too many details.

So, hold the popcorn. You don't have to pray all the time. You don't have to do all the talking. If you want to grow in your relationship with somebody, and you do all the talking, how much do you learn about the other person? *Nada*. Nothing, because you're too busy talking.

I think this is a kind of occupational hazard for us Catholics. We have so many beautiful rituals, so many beautiful, written prayers. So we sometimes tend to think,

> "Okay, I'm here to pray, so I guess I'd better pray. I'll pray a litany, and then I'll read this prayer, and then that prayer, and then I'll say a chaplet and then the rosary, etc., etc."

Now, I'm not telling you not to do those things, because they can be very meaningful. And we all have special prayers that we like to say. But don't fill all your Adoration time this way.

Our rituals, our written or memorized prayers, can become so familiar to us that, if we don't really work at it, we sometimes end up saying them without really thinking about what we're doing. As a result, instead of bringing us *closer* to God, saying a lot of rote prayers can actually be a way to *avoid personal contact* with God. I can be so busy "praying" that I fail to "hear" God, fail to reflect on thoughts that pop into my head, fail to recognize insights that God may be trying to give me. "Ah, don't bother me right now, God. I'm praying."

What are we avoiding? We are avoiding that face-to-face, intimate, beyond words relationship with God that's so vital if we want to grow spiritually. If I keep talking, I don't have to be afraid of that; I don't have to meet Him in that way; I don't have to deal with silence.

Silence can be really scary. If you're with other people, especially people you don't know very well, and there's silence for too long, it can get pretty intimidating, pretty awkward. We all tend to be afraid of that with God to some extent.

It's a fear that we can gradually grow out of by letting there be spaces of silence. You don't have to talk all the time! Dare to *just be there* with God. "Here I am, Lord." Dare to gaze upon Him without any words or conscious thoughts. I remember a poster I saw once. It said, "Sometimes I sits and thinks; sometimes I just sits." I always liked that.

Sometimes it's okay to come into the Adoration chapel and "just sit" with God. Back to St. Therese: "Prayer is a surge of the heart toward God." This can be more powerful than any words. If words help you let your heart surge towards God, then use them. But don't rely on them exclusively. Let there be spaces in the conversation, spaces of silence.

I talked earlier about using pictures for prayer intentions. But it doesn't have to be through pictures. If a thought or a person or a situation comes into your mind, just let your heart surge to God for that intention — a wordless surge towards God.

And dare to *listen*! "Okay, God, if You have anything You'd like to tell me, now's the time. Help me to hear You." It may not happen right away, but give Him the option now and then. Give Him some silent time when you're not talking at Him, so that if He wants to communicate something, He can.

Fr. George Kosicki taught me a variation of this, which he calls "Body Scream." He would just tune into his body and, whenever he felt especially tired or distracted or overwhelmed, he would find a place to sit or lie down and just let his body "scream." He wouldn't say anything; he wouldn't try to pray; he would just sit for a few minutes and let his body "breathe out" whatever stress was there.

We can do this in Adoration. Just sit in front of the Lord, take a slow, deep breath … "Okay, Lord, … Ahhhhhh." Just allow your body to let it all go, soundlessly, wordlessly to Him, present for you in the Eucharist.

FOR GOD'S SAKE, SHUT UP!

11

GO TO THE OFFICE!

No, not *your* office. This is not about work. It's about praying the form of prayer I mentioned back in Chapter 7: the *Liturgy of the Hours*, also known as the Breviary, or the Divine Office. It's the universal prayer of the Catholic Church, prayed daily by priests and religious all over the world.

More and more lay men and women are realizing that this prayer form is not exclusively reserved for priests and religious. In most religious congregations, they *have* to pray it at specific hours. We *get* to pray if we want to, and many people find it very fruitful.

There are several options. One is the full version, "The *Liturgy of the Hours*," which is a 4-volume set that follows each liturgical season of the Church. It can be a little confusing at first, so it helps if you begin by praying it with someone who is already used to it, and there's also a great little annual pocket *Guide to the Liturgy of the Hours* that gives you all the references and page numbers for the prayers designated for each day.

Or you can get a 1-volume version called *Christian Prayer*, which some people find a bit easier, at least to start with. Or you can subscribe to a little magazine called the *Magnificat*, which, in addition to Mass readings for each day, has abbreviated versions of some of the Hours.

Since you're not in a community with set rules for what has to be prayed when, you don't have to say it all. You can use it in whatever way works for you. You can decide to pray "The Office of Readings," or "Morning Prayer," or "Evening Prayer," or "Night Prayer," or any combination of them.

Many people have found that once they try it, they quickly grow to love it, especially because every time you pray it, you are joining the prayers of the entire Church. The prayers you're praying are being prayed every day by religious (and laity) all over the world. So you are entering into the universal prayer of the Church, prayer that is filled with beautiful scriptures, and with inspiring readings from the saints. It's a wonderful way to spend some of your Adoration time. Just pick one of the Hours, pray it in front of the Blessed Sacrament, and let the Lord speak to you through it.

GO TO THE OFFICE!

12

GET A TAN!

No, I'm not going to suggest that you wear your bathing suit to Adoration. But we can learn a lot about Adoration by thinking about what happens when we go out to sit in the sunshine and get a tan.

St. John of the Cross gives us a wonderful little analogy, in which he compares God to the sun:

> The sun is up early and shining on your house, ready to shine in if you open the curtains. So God, who never sleeps nor slumbers, ... is like the sun, shining over souls.
>
> LIVING FLAME, 46-7

Science tells us that the sun never sets, never "goes down." It's the earth that moves, turning away from the sun. The sun is still doing its thing. The sun is always shining. It gives light, it gives heat, it irradiates everything. That's what it does, all the time. You can't change that.

You can choose to put up an umbrella to block its light; you can choose to wander into a cave and wonder, "Why is it so cold and dark in here? Where did the sun go?" The sun didn't go anywhere; you did. It's still shining, still giving light and heat, still radiating. You simply can't feel any of that, because you have removed yourself from the sunlight.

I talk about this a lot when I speak about Confession, because one of the most important "secrets" about Confession is this:

Sin doesn't change God. It changes you.

Sin is when you move out of the Sonlight and into the darkness. Confession is coming out of the cave and back into the presence of God.

God is love and, in God, love is not a noun; it's a verb. Love is what God *does*, all the time. Just like the sun that is always shining, God is always loving you, always pouring His love upon you. You can't change that; your sin doesn't change that. He is always loving you, even when you sin. Nothing has the power to change God! He is always loving. That's simply what He does.

One of the greatest reminders of this for me is the Divine

Mercy Image, the picture of Christ with His right hand raised in blessing, His left hand inviting you into His heart, and the red and pale rays gushing forth from His pierced heart as a fountain of mercy for the world.

No matter how much you stare at that picture, you can't change it. You can't turn that right hand into a clenched fist. You can't turn it into an angry finger pointing at you. It's always blessing you. All you can do is either receive the blessing or reject it. You can't turn that inviting left hand into a hand that pushes you away. You can't dry up that outpouring stream of mercy.

If we could remove the veil of bread that conceals the Eucharistic presence of Jesus, this picture is what we would see. *The Eucharist is The Divine Mercy in Person*, the God who is always loving, always blessing, always inviting you deeper into His heart, always pouring His mercy upon you. When we come into Eucharistic Adoration we are placing ourselves in the path of those rays of mercy. We are Sonbathing.

When you go out in the sun to get a tan, you don't have to do anything in particular. The sun does it all. It *changes you.* You can read, listen to music, do some paperwork, or just lie there doing nothing. It doesn't matter what you do as long as you spend some time exposing yourself to the action of the sun.

The more often you do this, the more the desired change takes place, and the deeper your tan becomes. The only danger is the possibility of sunburn from too much sun too fast.

In Eucharistic Adoration there's no danger. God is always gentle. But the reality of change is the same. Whatever you do during your Adoration time, be aware of this reality and consciously open yourself to it, with gratitude and expectant faith. The more you expose yourself to the Eucharistic Heart of Jesus, the more His love will heal you, bless you, transform you, moment-by-moment. *Adoration is radiation therapy.* Here's a prayer that may help you get started:

Radiation Prayer

Lord, here I am. Thank You for being here and for letting me be with You. Lord, You know all my limitations, all my weakness. You know how hard it is for me to keep my focus on You. You know how mixed my motives can be, how confused I get sometimes.

But I am here, Lord, because I know I need You, and I want to be healed of everything that keeps me from being the person You created me to be.

So, I ask You, Lord, no matter what I'm able to do during this time — whether I pray or read, daydream or sleep, or just sit here in a seemingly mindless way — bless me, Lord, and work on me. Cleanse me, change me, mold me, remake me in Your image.

I am here to Son-bathe, Lord, to expose myself to the healing rays of Your love and become more like You. Please let it be done, hour by hour by hour.

© 2005 Vinny Flynn

GET A TAN!

13

FOR CRYING OUT LOUD!

Sometimes when I talk about Eucharistic Adoration, I ask, "How many of you have ever cried in front of the Eucharist?" I get pretty mixed reactions. Some people immediately nod their heads and raise their hands, and others look at me as if I'm crazy.

Maybe I am, but I've cried in front of the Eucharist many times, and it's always healing. Pope John Paul II says that God is a Father who "is always waiting for us to have recourse to Him in every need" (*Rich in Mercy*, #2). Not just big needs, but every need, from gaping wounds to the little scratches that just need a band aid or a loving parent to kiss the boo-boo.

God is not the kind of father who says, "Hey, stop your crying! Big boys don't cry." It's okay to cry out to God. When you go to Adoration, it's important to come before the Lord as you are, in your now moment. If you're in need, come with your need. If you're in distress come with your distress. If you feel like crying, cry. No words are necessary; just have a good cry. Be real with God! If you're alone in the chapel, cry out loud, even sob if you need to.

Obviously, if there are other people present, you need to be considerate of them and restrain yourself a little so as not to distract them from prayer. *But don't hide your pain from God.*

I remember, when my dad died, how strong my mother was. She was always there to hold the rest of us up when the grief hit us. I especially remember one moment when she was playing piano for me. I was trying to sing a song that my dad had often sung, and I got halfway through it and then just broke down and couldn't finish it. She never missed a beat. She picked up where I had left off and sang the rest of it herself.

But every morning after Mass, when all the other people had left, she would sit there with quiet tears streaming down her face. That was her time with God, when she could just let it all out. It was her time of healing.

Crying, when you have a reason to cry, is a physical, built-in repair mechanism that fosters the process of healing. Crying with someone who loves you increases that process and, since

God is the one who loves you most, crying in His presence brings the deepest healing.

There's no better place to bring your pain, no better shoulder to lean on, no better time to vent. Just keep remembering that God is your Father, and that He's "always waiting for you to have recourse to Him in every need."

14

SING A NEW SONG!

This is kind of an extension of the last chapter, in that it also centers on being real with God, being who you are with Him, and expressing yourself naturally and personally to Him. Like crying, it may be out of the comfort zone for some, but stretching your comfort zone can be a good thing.

If you are alone in Adoration and you like to sing, it's okay to sing to God. There's nothing irreverent about singing in front of the Eucharist. And it's very personal. It's virtually impossible for it not to be personal. Here you are, all alone with God, singing to Him.

If you get a chance, try it. It opens up a whole new dimension of direct, personal communication with God. As St. Augustine says, "He who sings prays twice."

If you're not alone during your time of adoration, there's another option. Find some other people who like to sing and find an appropriate time when either there are no others in the chapel, or they are willing to switch their time (or join you in song).

I remember a few years back, when my son Tim was a youth minister for a parish that had Perpetual Adoration, he got a group of young people together who liked to sing. They checked the schedule and found a time when there was no one there except one person. They went to that person, explained what they wanted to do, and asked if he would be willing to change his hour or join them if he wished.

He was okay with it, so every week they would gather for an hour of Adoration in song. Tim would bring his guitar, and they would spend the time together singing praise and worship songs to the Lord.

How pleased God must have been! What a wonderful way to honor God and offer back to Him the gifts He has given you.

As I write this, I'm reminded of the classic Christmas song "The Little Drummer Boy." The boy longed to honor the Christ Child, but had "no gift to bring that's fit to give our King." So, "to honor Him," he offered the gift he did have:

I played my drum for Him.
I played my best for Him.
Then He smiled at me,
Me and my drum.

As long as you are not disrupting the prayer of other people, it's okay to honor God's presence by expressing your love through music, to sing and play, to stand and praise Him, to lift your hands, to use your whole being to rejoice in His presence and exalt in Him:

Sing joyfully, O Israel!
Be glad and exalt with all your heart.
The Lord is in your midst.

ZEPH 3:14-15

A brief digression. At this point, I need to share a little story, a personal testimony of how God works in our lives and how perfect His timing can be. It concerns this theme of singing to the Lord and also the way God sometimes speaks clearly to us through the *Liturgy of the Hours* that I talked about in a previous chapter.

Yesterday, when I finished writing the first draft of this chapter, I felt that something was missing, so I decided that perhaps today I should look for a few more of the many scripture passages that encourage singing in the presence of the Lord. By this morning I had forgotten all about it, but the Lord was way ahead of me.

After morning Mass, I opened my breviary, as I do each day, to pray Morning Prayer before starting to write. The Canticle for today is from the book of Judith, and the scripture passage that precedes it is from Revelation 5:9:

They were singing a new song.

Remembering my resolution from yesterday, I smiled to myself (and to God) and read the Canticle. It starts like this:

Strike up the instruments,
A song to my God with timbrels,
chant to the Lord with cymbals.
Sing to him a new song,
Exalt and acclaim his name.
A new hymn I will sing to my God.

My smile got a lot bigger. Then I turned the page to read the Antiphon that follows:

Exult in God's presence with hymns of praise.

And after the Antiphon came Psalm 47:

All peoples, clap your hands,
Cry to God with shouts of joy. …

Sing praise to God, sing praise. …
Sing praise with all your skill.

So, in the spirit of the little drummer boy, remember that the greatest gift you can bring to lay before the King and honor Him is the gift of yourself — all you have and all you are. If music is a part of who you are, then sing a new song unto the Lord.

15

PRAY NOW AND THEN!

This is really not just a "tongue in cheek" title. It's a double pun that refers to two different ways of praying in the presence of God.

One way is kind of a spiritual adaptation of one of the main principles of Gestalt therapy. I call it "Praying the Gestalt." The principle is expressed in the short, simple phrase, "I, thou, here and now."

The basic concept is that, in your interactions with other people, it's important to stay in the present (instead of digging up the past) and to keep your communication direct and personal.

In its application to Eucharistic Adoration, it means that during your time in front of the Blessed Sacrament, you should strive to be present to the One who is present to you. How should you be present to Him? First of all, as we saw in the chapter entitled "Keep it personal," you should be present personally, as you are, one-on-one, person-to-person, just you and God (I, Thou). But you should also remain in the "here and now."

Don't get lost in reliving or regretting the past or in day-dreaming about the future. As I mentioned in the chapter on journaling, stay where you are, right now, at this moment, in this place. How are you feeling right now? What's going on with you right now? What's on your mind right now? What do you want to talk to God about right now? What do you want from God right now?

And remember that He's right here, right now, in person, loving you, wanting to bless you, wanting to talk to you.

> "Lord, thank You for being here. Thank You for loving me. What can I do to please You right now, Lord? What do You want to tell me right now?"

The other type of prayer referred to in the title is to use your *now* moment to pray *then*.

Huh???

There is no time with God. He lives in the Eternal Now. He's not limited by time and space as we are. We can only see things sequentially. We only know as much of the past as we can remember; we only discover the present, moment by moment; we can only imagine the future, but have to wait for it to reveal itself. Not so with God. For Him, past, present, and future are all one; He sees it all now.

So what? Three things. First, what Christ did *then* affects you *now*. Jesus, being God, was never subject to time and space. Some 2000 years ago, He looked out from the cross and saw you, right here, right now. He saw all your sin, all the stuff you wouldn't want anyone to see — and He loved you.

Then He reached across 2000 years of time and space and took all your sin into His pure body; and when that body was destroyed on the cross, your sin was destroyed, too. As the *Catechism of the Catholic Church* expresses it:

> Jesus knew and loved us each and all, during his life, his agony and his Passion, and gave himself up for each one of us.

#478

He died to save *you*, to win for you all the forgiveness and healing you will ever need. And what He won for you then is available to you in every now moment of your life, especially in the confessional. Through Confession, you access *now* the graces He won for you *then*.

Second thing: it works the other way around, too. It's not simply that what He did then affects you now. It's also that what *you* do now affected *Him* then.

Ever read any books or watch any science fiction films about traveling back through time and altering the past? Well, in a very real way, you can do it. He saw your sin, remember? But that's not all He saw. He saw all your good actions, words, and thoughts, too. He saw everything about you. He saw sins you haven't committed yet (and they hurt Him); but He also saw you stop to help an elderly woman cross the street *next week* (and that comforted Him).

What does all this mean? It means that at each now moment of your life, you can choose to either comfort and console Christ on the cross or add to His pain. You can pluck a thorn from His brow right now or push another in. Every time you sin, you hurt Him; and every time you do something good, you comfort Him.

This is the power you have to affect Christ's suffering, and it can be especially fruitful during Adoration. That same Christ who hung on the cross is present with you during your time of Adoration; and everything you think, say, do, or pray was present to Him when He was on the cross.

As you meditate on His sorrows, sympathize with His pain, try to please Him, try to accept His grace to become more like Him, you console Him on the cross, you lessen His agony, you diminish the suffering He would have felt if you were not spending this kind of time with Him right now. Every loving moment you spend with Him in Adoration comforts Him on the cross.

St. Faustina, through her frequent meditations on the Passion of Christ during times of Adoration, was so in touch with how much even her slightest sin hurt Jesus, that she determined to avoid committing even the least venial sin:

> Today, I entered into the bitterness of the Passion of the Lord Jesus. I suffered in a purely spiritual way. I learned how horrible sin was. God gave me to know the whole hideousness of sin. I learned in the depths of my soul how horrible sin was, even the smallest sin, and how much it tormented the soul of Jesus. I would rather suffer a thousand hells than commit even the smallest venial sin. ... I begged the Lord to grant me the grace of never consciously and deliberately offending Him by even the smallest sin or imperfection.
>
> *Diary*, 1016, 239

Third thing: Whatever you pray now, God hears then. Let me give you an example: When I heard that my brother Art had suffered a heart attack, I began to pray the Chaplet of Divine Mercy for him, and then later learned that he had already died before I started to pray. My prayer was too late.

No, it wasn't! It's never too late to pray, because God is not subject to time. He knows all things, all possibilities, past, present, and future. He knew about my prayer for Art even before either of us was born, and I firmly believe that He was with Art in a special way during the moments before He died, in answer to the prayer I hadn't prayed yet.

It's never too late to pray. Just say, "God, I didn't get to pray for this person, for this situation, for this intention, so I'm praying now. Please hear it then."

This is real! And it can be a great comfort, especially for those who have lost a loved one. Just lift that person up *now* and ask God to have been with him or her *then*.

PRAY NOW AND THEN!

16

GO TO YOUR TENT!

I guess I need to explain the title of this chapter. It's actually kind of a private joke between me and anyone who recognizes it as one of the comic lines from the Disney film *Mulan*. But it's also a pun that's meant to reflect the subject of this chapter, which is a prayer I call the "Tabernacle Prayer."

The word *tabernacle* is from the Latin word for tent, and it relates to the tabernacle that Moses erected in the wilderness as a portable dwelling place for the Lord. It was an extremely elaborate, movable temple in the desert, containing the Ark of the Covenant, altars of incense and burnt offerings, a laver for ceremonial washings, and the Tent of Meeting where the Lord would converse with Moses "face to face, as one man speaks to another" (Ex 33:11).

What I want to do in this chapter is invite you to "go to your tent," to enter the Tabernacle of the Most High and, as much as possible, meet Him face to face.

One day I got a phone call from a friend, who told me about a tragic situation that he and his wife were going through. It affected me very deeply. I felt so bad for them, so much grief, so much pain that my whole body felt sick. It got so bad that I couldn't think, I couldn't pray, and I felt I just had to lie down.

As I lay there I had a mental image of a tabernacle, and I felt drawn to approach it. In my mind I saw myself walk up to the tabernacle. The door opened, I stepped inside, and then the door closed behind me, and I heard the key turn in the lock.

A prayer rose within me:

> "Lord, lock me in the tabernacle with You. And let me bring them with me, Lord. Lock us in the tabernacle with You."

For a while, I just kept repeating that over and over. I wasn't aware of any other prayer or of any conscious thoughts. I lay there for about 20 minutes, and I don't have any clear memory of it, except that when I came to myself, everything was different. I don't think I was asleep; I was just wrapped in a deep peace. When I got up, I felt no sadness, no anxiety, no stress, just a quiet peace and trust in God.

Since then, this has become one of my favorite ways to pray, both for myself and in intercession for others. It's especially powerful when you are praying in front of the tabernacle when there is no Exposition of the Blessed Sacrament in a monstrance, or when you are not in a church at all but want to make a kind of spiritual communion. But you can also use it during your normal Holy Hour when the Sacrament is exposed in a monstrance. Just view the monstrance as a tabernacle.

For me, this has become a special way of uniting myself with the Eucharistic presence of Christ. There's something so comforting, so healing about this image — to leave the turmoil of the world for a time; to lay aside all the problems, worries, burdens of the day and enter the quiet peacefulness of that sanctuary; to feel the door shut out everything else and leave me safe and secure in the Eucharistic embrace of God.

It reminds me of a scene that Longfellow created in the first section of his poem *Divinia Commedia*. He writes of a workman who pauses from his work, sets down his burden, and enters a cathedral to pray, shutting out the noises of the world for a time to experience the peace of God:

> Oft have I seen at some cathedral door
> A laborer, pausing in the dust and heat,
> Lay down his burden,
> and with reverent feet

Enter, and cross himself,
and on the floor
Kneel to repeat his paternoster o'er;
Far off the noises of the world retreat;
The loud vociferations of the street
Become an undistinguishable roar.

Now, anytime I feel that the world is getting to me too much, anytime I start to feel too overwhelmed, too burdened, too anxious, too depressed, too exhausted, too caught up in myself, I just mentally approach the tabernacle and ask Jesus to lock me in there with Him. There, once again, I experience the peace that passes understanding, the peace that only God can give. There I remember, "Oh, yeah, You're God. You are all that I need. You can handle everything."

As St. Faustina writes,

O Prisoner of Love, I lock up my poor heart in this tabernacle, that it may adore You without cease night and day. … On leaving the earth, O Lord, You wanted to stay with us, and so You left us Yourself in the Sacrament of the Altar, and You opened wide Your mercy to us. There is no misery that could exhaust You; You have called us all to this fountain of love, to this spring of God's compassion. Here is the tabernacle of Your mercy, here is the remedy for all our ills.

DIARY, 80, 1747

GO TO YOUR TENT!

17

USE THE THREE R's!

In Deuteronomy 11:26, we hear Moses proclaim to the people, "I set before you here, this day, a blessing and a curse." And again in 30:19, "I have set before you life and death, the blessing and the curse. Choose life."

There are many things we could draw from these passages and from the context in which they were spoken. But here I simply want to call your attention to one truth that these passages express: There is a direct relationship between life and blessing and between death and cursing; and we are called to choose life.

The *Catechism* confirms this, telling us that "Blessing is a divine and life-giving action, the source of which is the Father."

It goes on to explain that, from the beginning of creation, "God blessed all living beings, especially man and woman," but sin "brought a curse upon the ground." In spite of this, God made a covenant with Noah and "renewed this blessing."

Later, God said to Abraham, "I will bless you … so that you may be a blessing" (Gen 12:2). Abraham embraced this blessing and, thus, "with Abraham, the divine blessing entered into human history which was moving toward death, to redirect it toward life" (See *Catechism*, 1078-1080).

Get the message? God blesses us, which is "life-giving," so that we can pass on that blessing to others, and thus help foster the culture of life instead of the culture of death. In Romans 12:14, St. Paul makes this really clear, "Bless and do not curse." And St. Peter adds:

> Do not return evil for evil, or insult for insult; but, on the contrary, a blessing, because to this you were called, that you might inherit a blessing. For: "Whoever would love life and see good days must keep the tongue from evil and the lips from speaking deceit, must turn from evil and do good, seek peace and follow after it."
>
> 1 PET 3:9-11

"Keep the tongue from evil" — ah, that's often the problem. (Don't worry, I *will* get to the three R's.) As St. James tells us, the tongue is just a "small member" of the body, but it can become "a restless evil, full of deadly poison. With it we bless the Lord and Father, and with it we curse human beings who are made in the likeness of God. From the same mouth come blessing and cursing. This need not be so" (3:8-10).

How about *your* mouth? Do you only use it to bless, or also, at times, to curse?

At every intersection of our daily lives, you and I are presented with a choice. In this situation, this circumstance, this encounter with another person, am I going to respond with a blessing or a curse? Am I going to be a light in the darkness, or am I going to curse the darkness and thus become part of it?

Well, I have a confession to make. I make the wrong response virtually every day, sometimes even several times a day. And my guess is, so do you. Why? Because we don't live in a perfect world. Not everyone is nice to us all the time.

Let's face it, we are all often hurt by people who don't treat us the way we should be treated, people who just aren't there when we need them to be, people who are inconsiderate, demanding, unreasonable, undependable, arrogant, critical, dishonest, and even downright nasty.

And sometimes life seems to kick us in the teeth through events, situations, and circumstances that we can't control and that leave us disappointed, frustrated, angry, and depressed.

How do we tend to react? With anger, resentment, bitterness, judgment, and a bunch of other not so pleasant thoughts and feelings. At times this results in sins of the tongue, and we say some pretty harsh things. But at other times — many other times — we don't say anything, at least not out loud. We don't sin with the tongue; we sin with our minds and our hearts. We "say" things inside ourselves. As I discussed in the chapter about evicting unwanted tenants, some pretty negative stuff can make its way into our hearts, and often it all just sits inside us and festers, like cancerous sores that eat away at us.

What does all this really come down to? Unforgiveness. All these negative thoughts, words, feelings, and judgments are really forms of unforgiveness, and we need to get rid of them. As St. Paul exhorts us:

> Get rid of all bitterness, all passion and anger, harsh words, slander, and malice of every kind. In place of these, be kind to one another, compassionate, and mutually forgiving.
>
> EPH 4:31-32

So we not only need to get rid of all these things (curses); we also need to put something else in their place (blessings). How do we do it? (I thought you'd never ask!) — *By using the Three R's.*

The Three R's are:

1. Repent
2. Revoke
3. Replace.

You're driving down the road, when suddenly someone cuts you off, and you have to slam on your brakes. You growl inside, your body tenses up, and your face turns into a snarl: "What a jerk! Why don't you learn how to drive?" Gradually you start to relax, and then you realize that you just chose to curse instead of to bless. What do you do? Use the Three R's:

    1. Repent. "Oh, Lord, there I go again. I'm sorry, Lord. I repent of that reaction; I repent of the thoughts, the judgments, the anger, the words I uttered."

    2. Revoke. "I revoke all those negative, unkind thoughts, Lord. I un-think them, and I un-say those words."

    3. Replace. "I replace those 'curses' with a blessing, Lord. I forgive him, and I bless him, and I ask that You bless him, Lord."

My son-in-law Jason Free gives another great example in his book *Parenting on Purpose.* He was explaining that he had gotten his family in the habit of reminding each other to live the scriptural passage from Ephesians 4:29: "Let no evil talk come out of your mouths, but only what is useful for building up … so that your words may give grace to those who hear." He called it the "4:29 Challenge." Whoever heard another member of the family using the tongue to curse instead of bless would shout out "4:29!" Here's the story he shared:

I'm driving my family home from church and without even realizing it, I blurt out a sarcastic comment about the soloist in the choir loft. "4:29!" somebody shouts from the rear of the car. I feel like I was just pelted by a spiritual dodge ball. "Unbelievable," I mutter in total annoyance with myself. "Five minutes out of church and my tongue is already a loose cannon."

How does he react? With the Three R's:

1. Repent. "Lord, I'm so sorry. I can't believe I just made a useless comment about that person. And I did it in front of my kids. I don't want to be that kind of example, Lord. It's so arrogant to speak that way. I fully repent of it, Lord."

2. Revoke. "Lord, I revoke what I said. I un-say it. I spiritually take those worthless words back. I don't want them falling on anyone else."

3. Replace. "Lord, I replace those words with a blessing. I thank you for this woman. You love her just as much as you love me and my kids. Help me to remember that. I bless her, Lord. I bless her life and her heart that sings to you. Please bless her, God."

You can use the Three R's anytime, anyplace, but it's especially fruitful in Eucharistic Adoration. You just sit there in front of the Blessed Sacrament and ask Jesus to heal you of any unforgiveness that you're hanging onto. As memories come to mind, or as you recognize any negative stuff inside you, just repent, revoke, and replace it in the presence of the Lord.

18

GIVE IT UP!

In the first two chapters I talked about some different ways of "unloading," clearing your mind and heart of anything that might keep you from really entering into union with Christ in Adoration.

Here I want to suggest some tools you can use to "unload" when you really feel overwhelmed, with so many things on your mind, so many things to do, so many little or big problems weighing you down, that you feel helpless.

And I also want to give you an example of the kinds of things that can come from the habit of journaling that I talked about back in Chapter 5.

The first tool is very simple: *Stop trying to do it all yourself!* As the Lord confided to St. Faustina when she couldn't figure out why she was having such trouble keeping her resolutions, **"You were counting too much on yourself and too little on me"** (*Diary*, 1087).

Whatever's on your mind, whatever's weighing you down, whatever's going on that makes you feel helpless or hopeless, you don't have to carry it; you don't have to hang onto it. Just acknowledge it, admit your powerlessness, and give it up to God.

My main confessor has a great, easy-to-remember prayer for this. You simply say to the Lord:

I can't. You can. I think I'll let You.

Memorize this! It won't take long, and it will be well worth the time. Such a powerful little phrase! Such a great reminder: "Oh, yeah. I'm not God; You are!"

In addition to teaching people how to use this simple little prayer, he also sometimes suggests using a series of mental images that can help you let it all go. You start by closing your eyes and looking inside yourself. What's on your mind right now? What things are burdening you? Gather them all together into a blob in your mind. You can even give the blob a name; my "Grief," my "Worries," my "Problems," my "Stuff," my "Misery."

Then you try to really see it. What does this blob look like?

What size is it? What shape is it? What color is it? Is it light? Is it heavy? Is it soft? Is it hard? Now try to imagine seeing yourself taking this blob into your hands, feeling its weight, and then handing it to Jesus and watching Him take it.

It doesn't work for everybody, but for people who can visualize mental images like this, it really helps to take specific things, create a picture of them in your mind, and see yourself handing them to God.

Another image that I have found helpful is the image of chains. Wounds are chains. Sins are chains. Worries and anxieties are chains. They come in all different lengths and weights, but they're all chains, and they weigh us down. St. Paul talks about the spiritual life as "running the race" (See 2 Tim 4:7). Well, I can't run a good race if I've got chains hanging around my neck. Sometimes I'm carrying so many chains that I can barely walk.

So I imagine Christ reaching down from the cross and saying, "Give them to me." I see myself giving them to Him, and watching Him put them around His own neck and stretch out His arms on the cross once again.

This isn't just imagining. It's what Christ really did on the cross. He took all our chains and smashed them to free us:

> Some lay in darkness and in gloom,
> prisoners in misery and chains. ...
> Then they cried to the Lord

in their need,
and he rescued them
from their distress.
He led them forth
from darkness and gloom
and broke their chains to pieces.

Psalm 107

We don't have to keep hanging onto our chains. We need to give them to God and let them go.

I remember one time in particular when I was feeling especially overwhelmed. I was starting to write in my journal in front of the Blessed Sacrament, and I just began by complaining to the Lord, "Oh, God, there's just so much! So I put it all into your hands right now ..." Then I started listing things, and the list went on for two pages — so much to do, so many projects unfinished, so many people needing prayer, so much to think about, meetings, financial concerns, family concerns, and on and on.

Now I really felt overwhelmed! The image of putting it into His hands just wasn't working for me, and a different image came to mind, so I wrote:

> "Lord, I'm trying to give this all to You, but this is way too much for me to hold in my hands and place into Yours. So I place all this stuff in a dump truck and back it up to the abyss of Your mercy and dump it into Your keeping, Lord."

As I wrote, still another image came to mind.

> "No, Lord, it's still not enough, so I load it all, piece by piece into a big trailer truck and back it up to the loading dock of Your love. It's all Yours now, Lord, the whole truckload. I transfer all ownership to You. Don't let me try to take any of it back. You sort it, trash anything You don't want, rewrite my scripts, redefine my goals, prioritize them, and hand back the things You want me to do. Help me to treat each of them as Your projects, Lord, not mine."

When I finished writing, I felt empty, and relaxed, and free, with a new sense of trust in God. So I jotted down one more line: "Time for Mass, Lord. Thank You." Then I left the little Adoration chapel to go into the main church for Mass.

As I walked around the corner of the building, I had a view of the main street, and I watched in amazement as a huge trailer truck pulled up right in front of me and stopped for a moment to let someone cross the street. On the side of the truck was a big sign that said:

Truckload: Key to Success

I started to laugh and thought, "What a sense of humor You have, Lord! Okay, I think I get the message!"

19

GET WITH THE PROGRAM!

I remember waking up once in the middle of the night and getting an awful, sinking feeling that someone was about to get into a car accident. I immediately thought of my kids and started trying to remember who was still out, but then I realized that they were all home. So it wasn't my kids. But I felt strongly that it was somebody's kids, that they were in danger, and that God was calling me to pray for them.

I realized, of course, that no matter how strong this "premonition" was, it could just be my imagination. But I figured, "What's it going to hurt if I pray for whomever God might want me to pray for?" So I began to pray in whatever ways came to mind, and I continued until the feeling left me and I felt calm. I never did find out who I was praying for, but it didn't matter. I felt that God had invited me to participate in His mercy, and it felt good.

Some time later, I was introduced to a type of prayer that reminded me of this. It's a form of intercessory prayer where we finally stop asking God for the things we want. We stop petitioning God. In other words, we stop praying for ourselves, and for our families, and for our friends, and for our work, and for our needs, and for more money, and all the other things we ask God for most of the time.

Instead, we just try to empty ourselves, quiet all the insistent voices in our minds, focus on Jesus present before us, and say, "Okay, God, enough about *me*. What's on Your mind? What do *You* want me to pray for?" It's when you try to set aside your own agendas for a time and tune into God's.

This type of prayer is especially powerful when you do it with other people in a group, but you can also do it on your own. I call it "Blank Screen Prayer," because you're letting your mind become a blank screen as much as possible, so that God can project something onto it. You're not choosing who to intercede for; you're letting *God* do that. Sometimes, you don't even know who you're praying for, and you don't need to know. It can be anyone, anywhere.

It's a very quiet, unhurried, mostly silent way of praying,

a breaking free from self-absorption, a patient listening, a willingness to intercede with Christ for His intentions. You don't actively try to find anything to pray for; you just try to be open to whatever God may lead you to. A thought may pop into your head, or a picture, a song, an idea, a place, a person, a memory, and you just let your mind go with it. Sometimes very specific intentions come to mind; sometimes nothing.

I remember once when my wife and I were praying together in this way, and she suddenly got a mental image of a girl in China. That's all; nothing else. But it was a very clear image. So we spent some time praying for a girl in China, asking God to bless her and whatever her situation was.

If nothing comes, that's okay, too. You're offering the time to God for whatever He wants. Your prayer is a *prayer of presence*, of being with God, not for yourself, but for Him; and He can use your self-offering as prayer for whatever or whomever He chooses.

The Christian agenda is to come to want what God wants. Well, sometimes I want to want what God wants, but I haven't gotten there yet; I'm still too attached to my own wants. But that's the goal for all of us who call ourselves Christians. And this type of prayer can help us to finally get to that goal, where all we want is to please Him, all we want is to participate in *His* agenda.

20

GO FOR THE GRITS!

If you have read my book *7 Secrets of the Eucharist*, you may remember that I devoted the Afterword to Fr. Hal Cohen, a wonderful Jesuit priest from New Orleans. Fr. Hal was brought up in the south and, from the time he was a baby, he loved grits. According to his parents, his first word wasn't *ma-ma* or *da-da*. It was *more*, and what he wanted more of was grits.

Later on in his life, that word *more* took on a powerful new meaning for him. He had come to realize that no matter how many graces we receive, God always has more to give, and He *wants* to give it. He just waits for us to ask.

So, in the last years of his life, Fr. Hal, once greedy for grits, became greedy for grace, and the prayer most often on his lips was "More, Lord, more." He used to love a section of St. Faustina's diary that he called "Gathering the Gems." It's a vision she had where she saw people gathering graces from the Heart of Jesus:

> Today I saw the Crucified Lord Jesus. Precious pearls and diamonds were pouring forth from the wound in His Heart. I saw how a multitude of souls was gathering these gifts, but there was one soul who was closest to His Heart and she, knowing the greatness of these gifts, was gathering them with liberality, not only for herself, but for others as well. The Savior said to me, **Behold, the treasures of grace that flow down upon souls, but not all souls know how to take advantage of My generosity**.
>
> *DIARY*, 1687

At another time, He complained to her that some people are not willing to receive His graces:

> The Lord said to me, **I want to give myself to souls and to fill them with My love, but few there are who want to accept all the graces My love has intended for them. My grace is not lost; if the soul for whom it was intended does not accept it, another soul takes it**.
>
> *DIARY*, 1017

Are you reluctant to ask because you feel you're not worthy? Of course you're not worthy! None of us are worthy; none of us deserve God's love. But that doesn't stop Him. He is rich in mercy. What's mercy? It's undeserved love, and God wants to pour it out upon us. So, it's not only okay to be greedy for grace; it's the way God wants us to be. He told Saint Faustina:

> **Act like a beggar who does not back away when he gets more alms [than he asked for], but offers thanks the more fervently. You too should not back away and say that you are not worthy of receiving greater graces when I give them to you. I know you are unworthy, but rejoice all the more and take as many treasures from My Heart as you can carry, for then you will please Me more. And I will tell you one more thing: Take these graces not only for yourself, but also for others.**
>
> *DIARY*, 294

When you're in front of the Blessed Sacrament, don't be afraid to ask for more, for yourself, for your loved ones — and let Him know that you're willing to take even the graces that have been refused by others. Christ is right there with you, waiting for you to ask, so He can pour out more and more graces, far more precious than pearls and diamonds. Like Fr. Hal, go for more spiritual grits.

TAKE A SHOWER!

In Chapter 12, I mentioned the Divine Mercy Image and explained that it can be seen as a representation of the Eucharistic presence of Jesus pouring His mercy upon us. I suggested that one powerful form of imaging prayer is to imagine ourselves "Sonbathing" in those rays of mercy.

In this chapter I want to present another image, the image of those rays as an endless fountain, an outpouring shower of mercy in which we can actually bathe.

Scripture is filled with images of water, especially prophetic images of Christ and His Church as the source of an endless "fountain of life" being poured out upon creation:

A fountain shall issue from the house of the Lord" (Joel 3:18), ... a fountain of life (Ps 36:9) ... a fountain to purify from sin and uncleanness (Zec 13:1), ... a spring of water welling up to eternal life (Jn 4:14), ... life-giving water, sparkling like crystal, flowing from the throne of God and of the Lamb (Rev 22:1).

All these, I believe, point to a single event, the dramatic event recorded in the Gospel of St. John, when the centurion pierced the heart of Jesus with a lance, "and immediately blood and water flowed out" (19:34) — a fountain of mercy, now and forever available for all who come to draw "living water" from it.

If you have seen the film *The Passion of the Christ*, you may remember how dramatically and graphically this scene is presented. As the centurion thrusts the lance into the Heart of Jesus, a gushing stream of blood and water bursts forth and showers down upon the centurion and upon John and Mary at the foot of the cross. They are completely drenched in that outpouring fountain of mercy.

As you gaze upon the Eucharist in the Adoration chapel, you can pray a prayer of immersion, imagining yourself standing under the fountain of love streaming from the Host, standing with Mary at the foot of the cross, allowing the blood and water to shower upon you, cleansing, purifying, forgiving, healing, and restoring. If you're praying for others, you can mentally immerse them in that endless fountain.

You can continue to use this kind of immersion prayer at other times as well. It has become such a powerful image for me that I use it in all kinds of ways. When I get caught in the rain, I pray that it will signify a new shower of grace to draw me closer to God.

When I water the vegetables in my garden to keep them alive and growing, I use it as intercessory prayer, asking God to immerse my children in the fountain of His love.

When I take my morning shower, I pray that each drop of water will be like the blood and water that poured from His Heart, that those "drops" of mercy will penetrate into my whole being — my mind, my heart, my soul, my memories, my emotions — and remove anything unclean, any "dirt," any sin, any leftover imprint of sin, anything that might draw me away from God.

In the last chapter I talked about asking for more, being greedy for grace. This type of imaging prayer is a perfect way to do that. When we approach God in this way, trusting in His love, He really does shower us with grace, more and more. As Christ said to Faustina:

> **Take the vessel of trust and draw from the fountain of life — for yourself, but also for other souls. … I have opened My Heart as a living fountain of mercy. Let all souls draw life from it. … The more a**

soul trusts, the more it will receive. Souls that trust boundlessly are a great comfort to Me, because I pour all the treasures of My graces into them.

DIARY, 1488, 1520, 1578

TAKE A SHOWER!

IMPROVE YOUR IMAGE!

I want to talk about beginnings and endings. If you've made it this far, through all "21 Ways," you may be thinking that this Afterword is the end of the book. But it's not supposed to be an ending; the whole book is supposed to be a beginning.

Let's start with the title. There's no magic about the number 21; I just liked the alliterative sound when it's combined with Ways and Worship. And, obviously there are more than 21 ways.

That's where you come in. I've given you 21 ways just to "prime the pump," so to speak, to "kick start your engine." Each chapter is meant to give you a starting place, to let you experiment with an idea, a technique, a prayer, so that you can see what works best for you — and then, hopefully, be inspired to move on from there, adding your own variations, your own prayers.

In the actual beginning of the book, the Foreword, I explained that the whole purpose of the Eucharist, and thus, of Eucharistic Adoration, is union with God. That's the "end" that we should keep in mind right from the beginning. The goal of our worship is to come to know God so personally and completely that we become one with Him.

But why? Why do want to do this? Why does *God* want us to do this? Why would He want us to praise Him, thank Him, adore Him, worship Him? Is he on some kind of ego trip? Does he need our praise, our applause? Is He insecure and just needs a little affirmation, a little pat on the shoulder?

Of course not. In one of the options for weekday Mass, there's a beautiful prayer in the Eucharistic Preface, where the priest says to God:

> You have no need of our praise, yet our desire to thank you is itself your gift. Our prayer of thanksgiving adds nothing to your greatness, but makes us grow in your grace, through Jesus Christ our Lord.

We don't worship God because *He* needs it; we worship Him because *we* need it. God — and God alone — is infinitely worthy of our praise; and His mercy and majesty are certainly more than reason enough for us to praise Him. But He is so generous, so loving, that He uses even our worship of Him to help *us*. When we worship Him, *we* grow. How do we grow? Through the same principle we can see at work even in our secular culture:

We become what we worship!

We see this, for example, when people begin to "idolize" particular TV personalities, film stars, musicians, superheros, or top models in fashion magazines and reality shows. What happens? Gradually, but continually, they start to talk like them, dress like them, look like them, act like them. They do everything possible to be like them, even, in some cases, to the extent of getting a makeover. (I almost decided to title this Afterword "Get a Makeover!")

Why worship God? Because the more we worship Him, the more we become *like* Him — we get an extreme makeover. Why do we want to be like Him? Well, for that we need to go back to the very beginning. In Genesis, the first book of the Bible, we're told that "in the beginning" God created us in "His image and likeness" (1:26-27). Why? Because God is love, and love longs to give of itself.

You and I exist because God wanted more children to love, to bless, to unite with Himself and fill them with eternal joy. The end that God had in mind from the beginning is that someday He wants to introduce you and me into the Trinity itself to be one with Him forever. As the *Catechism* expresses it:

> The ultimate end ... is the entry of God's creatures
> into the perfect unity of the Blessed Trinity.
>
> #260

But there's a problem. Sin has disfigured us so that, though we remain in the image of God, we have lost our likeness to Him (See *Catechism*, # 705). We don't *look* like Him anymore, we don't *act* like Him, we don't *think* like Him, we don't *see* things (or other people) the way He sees them.

Fortunately, God didn't decide to throw away this batch of sinful clay and start over. Instead, He sent His Son Jesus to assume our human image and "restore it in the Father's likeness" (#705).

How? By His sacrifice on the cross. But it didn't end there. It wasn't a "quick fix." It was grace made available. Remember the Eternal Now from Chapter 15? What He did then affects us now.

Pope John Paul II teaches that Christ's suffering and death on the cross are "concentrated forever in the Eucharist" (*The Church of the Eucharist*, #5). Thus, through our reception and adoration of the Eucharist, we receive the fruits of Christ's sacrifice and are restored in God's likeness now, moment by moment. It's a process!

He goes on to refer to the Eucharist as "a mode of being,"

which passes from Jesus into each of us and is meant to pass from us into the world (See *Stay with us Lord*, #25). In the Eucharist, it's as if Christ is saying, "Here's my way of living, my way of being, my thoughts, my feelings, my attitudes, my values, my perceptions, my way of seeing the world, my way of loving. Take it all into yourself and pass it on."

Pope Benedict XVI picks up this theme and runs with it, explaining that through our regular reception and adoration of the Eucharist we gradually take on Christ's whole way of being and experience a "radical newness" that transfigures every aspect of our lives. Everything is brought into conformity with Christ; our thoughts, our words, our feelings, our actions. He calls this process the "progressive transfiguration of all those called by grace to reflect the image of the Son of God ... " (*The Sacrament of Charity*, #71).

"To reflect the image." In Chapter 12, when I was talking about the Eucharist radiating and changing us, I mentioned that, if we could see beyond the veil of what looks like bread, what we would see is the Divine Mercy Image — Jesus Himself blessing us, inviting us into His heart, and pouring His grace into us. Through our Eucharistic Adoration we are supposed to *become* that image, to become *like* God. Remember His plan to introduce us into the Trinity with Him? We can't be *with* Him until we're *like* Him, so we need to allow His Eucharistic "mode of being" to penetrate our lives and gradually transform us so that, like Our Lady, we will become transparent to God and radiate His love to others.

The hours you spend in front of the Blessed Sacrament are not just isolated pieces of time. They are part of a continuing process, "a process leading ultimately to the transfiguration of the entire world" (*The Sacrament of Charity*, #11). So your time in Adoration is not insignificant. It's immensely important, for you, for the Church, for the world. Even more than that — it's vital. And it's not separate and unrelated to my time in Adoration. Individually and together we are committing to allow Christ to change us so completely that, through us, He can change the world.

The transformation of the world will come when enough of us, through our regular reception of the Eucharist and our hours of Adoration, become so changed, so transfigured that we can say with St. Paul, "It is no longer I who live, but Christ lives in me" (Gal 2:20). We then become "living Eucharist." We become the Divine Mercy Image in the world, allowing Christ, who now lives in us, to radiate His love into all whom we meet, moment by moment, day by day.

AFTERWORD: IMPROVE YOUR IMAGE!

ADDITIONAL PRAYERS FOR ADORATION

A selection of prayers by Vinny Flynn (VF) and Erin Flynn (EF)

My God,
I believe that You are truly present here
under the appearance of bread.
Help me now to be present to You
and open myself fully to receive Your love.

VF

Ezekiel Prayer

Come now, Lord,
and sprinkle clean water upon me.
Cleanse me from all my impurities
and from all my idols.
Give me a new heart and place a new spirit within me,
taking away my stony heart
and giving me a natural heart.
Put Your Spirit within me, Lord,
so that I may live by Your statutes,
and carefully observe Your decrees.

VF (ADAPTED FROM EZEKIEL 36:25-27)

Father God,
You are indeed a Father "rich in mercy,"
slow to anger, gracious and compassionate
to all who call upon You.
In praise and thanksgiving,
I offer this day to You.
In the name of Jesus,
and in union with Mary Immaculate,
St. Faustina, and all the saints and angels,
I ask for the grace to become
a living image of Your love,
a living monstrance of Your presence,
empowered by Your Holy Spirit
to call down Your blessing
upon all the people and all the situations
I encounter today
as an instrument of Your mercy.

VF

"Father of unfailing light,
give that same light to me
as I call upon You.
May my lips praise You,
My life proclaim Your goodness,
my work give You honor,
and my voice celebrate You forever.

VF (ADAPTED FROM THE DIVINE OFFICE,
PRAYER AFTER THE PSALM,
MORNING PRAYER, SUNDAY OF WEEK I)

Spiritual Communion

Jesus, as always my mind and heart
are pulled in so many directions.
In this moment … here … now…
I remove myself from the noise,
and enter the quiet of eternity.
I unite myself to Your Eucharistic Presence,
as You sit, loving us
from all the tabernacles of the world.

Lord I cannot receive You now in Holy Communion,
but I long to be filled with You just the same.
I open myself to You completely;
to Your power, to Your wisdom, to Your love.
Let everything I am
be transformed
by everything You are.
I re-consecrate this day to You
so that every thought, word, and deed
will be filled with Your Presence.

EF

Philippians Prayer

Help me, Lord, to rejoice in You always,
with no anxiety about anything.
In everything,
by prayer and supplication
with thanksgiving
let me make my requests
known to You.

VF (Adapted from Philippians 4:4,6)

Lord Jesus, I place all my trust in You,
and I will follow You as Your disciple
every day of my life.
I repent of all my sins,
even the tiniest sins,
all the ways I have turned from You
or failed to reflect Your love to others.
I revoke any thoughts or words
that have been negative, judgmental, or unkind,
and I replace them with blessing.
I forgive all who have ever hurt me
and I ask You
to bless them with Your love.
Lord Jesus, by the healing power
of Your Eucharistic presence,
restore me in Your image and likeness
so that I may live like You and with You forever.

VF

Petition

I come with a heart full of petitions
A heart breaking with the heaviness
Of so much need.

But as I receive You, Jesus, I am silent.
I know it is good to ask,
That You love a generous and selfless soul.
But let my asking be but a motion now.
I move within and meet You, entering Your heart
And with me come all those I care for,
All I have enclosed in my heart

My love can only do them so much good,
But I nestle close
to feel the breathing of Your love
The rhythmic beats of union
As my heart melts into Yours

And they sit with me here
Resting — resting.

I bring them to bask in the Presence
Of the One who can meet
All their needs.

EF

Mary, as I kneel here
in the presence of your Son Jesus,
I turn to you
to help me adore Him more completely.
Wherever Jesus is, you are with Him.
It is thanks to your "fiat,"
your offering of your own body
in sheer abandonment to God,
that the Word became flesh in your womb.
This was the first reception of Holy Communion,
and when you gave birth to the Son of God,
you were the first to adore His presence among us.
Throughout your life you remained in communion
    with your Son,
always united with Him in unselfish love.
Teach me, Mary, how to adore Him as you do,
how to remain always in His presence
in complete union with His holy will.

VF (Based on the Message of Pope John Paul II, 8/15/96)

Overflow

What use is it if I receive You
and do not bear You to the world?
   "Mary went in haste ..."
What use is it if I join myself to You in love
and do not love my brother?
   "They'll know you are my disciples ..."
Is it even possible to be truly united to Goodness
and not share that goodness?

What kind of union is it, if I stay my same self thereafter?
Do not allow me to remain as I am, Jesus.
Help me to prepare my heart for true union with You,
a union that will reveal You to the world uniquely through me.

For what use is it if You come to me and I refuse You
   to my neighbor?
What use is it, Lord, if You fill me and I do not overflow?

EF

Loving Father,
may everything I do today
begin with Your inspiration
and continue with Your saving help.
May my work always find its origin in You
and, through You, reach completion.

VF (ADAPTED FROM THE DIVINE OFFICE,
CLOSING PRAYER OF MORNING PRAYER, WEEK I)

ADDITIONAL PRAYERS FOR ADORATION

RECOMMENDED BOOKS AND RESOURCES

Eucharistic

7 Secrets of the Eucharist.
   Vinny Flynn. MercySong/Ignatius.

For the Life of the World: Saint Maximilian and the Eucharist.
   Jerzy Domanski, OFM Conv. Translated by Fr. Peter D.
   Fehlner, FI. Academy of the Immaculate.

God is Near Us: The Eucharist, the Heart of Life.
   Joseph Cardinal Ratzinger (Pope Benedict XVI).
   Ignatius Press.

Jesus Our Eucharistic Love.
   Fr. Stefano M. Manelli, FFI.
   Franciscan Friars of the Immaculate.

My Daily Eucharist. Vols. I & II.
Meditations for each day, compiled and edited by
Joan Carter McHugh. Witness Ministries.

*Praying in the Presence of Our Lord: Prayers for
Eucharistic Adoration.*
Fr. Benedict J. Groeschel, C.F.R. Our Sunday Visitor.

*Rekindle Eucharistic Amazement: Healing and Holiness through
the Mass and Holy Hour.*
Kathleen Beckman. Queenship Publishing

Sacrament of Charity.
Apostolic Exhortation of Pope Benedict XVI.
Pauline Books & Media.

Stay With Us, Lord.
Apostolic Letter of Pope John Paul II.
Pauline Books & Media.

*Study Guide for 7 Secrets of the Eucharist: Encountering the
Heart of God.*
Mary Flynn. MercySong/Ignatius.

The Church of the Eucharist.
Encyclical Letter of Pope John Paul II.
Pauline Books & Media.

The Eucharist and The Trinity.
M.V. Bernadot, OP. Michael Glazier, Inc.

With Burning Hearts: A Meditation on the Eucharistic Life.
   Henri J.M. Nouwen. Orbis Books.

Divine Mercy

Divine Mercy in My Soul.
   The Diary of Saint Maria Faustina Kowalska. Marian Press.

Faustina: Saint for Our Times.
   Fr. George W. Kosicki, CSB, with David Came.
   Marian Press.

Now is the Time for Mercy.
   Fr. George W. Kosicki, CSB and Vinny Flynn.
   Marian Press.

Pope Benedict's Divine Mercy Mandate.
   David Came. Marian Press.

Rich in Mercy.
   Encyclical Letter of Pope John Paul II.
   Pauline Books & Media.

Marian

*33 Days to Morning Glory: A Do-it-Yourself Retreat in
   Preparation for Marian Consecration.*
   Fr. Michael Gaitley, MIC. Marian Press.

Hail Holy Queen: The Mother of God in the Word of God.
   Scott Hahn. Doubleday.

John Paul II's Book of Mary.
  Compiled by Margaret R. Bunson. Our Sunday Visitor.

Mary in an Adult Church: Beyond Devotion to Response.
  Fr. David Knight. His Way Communications.

Mary: God's Yes to Man.
  John Paul's Encyclical "Redemptoris Mater."
  Intro by Joseph Cardinal Ratzinger. Ignatius Press.

Prayer Books

A Catholic Woman's Book of Prayers.
  Donna-Marie Cooper O'Boyle. Our Sunday Visitor.

*Catholic Saints Prayer Book: Moments of Inspiration from
  Your Favorite Saints.*
  Donna-Marie Cooper O'Boyle. Our Sunday Visitor.

Christian Prayer: Liturgy of the Hours.
  Catholic Book Publishing Co.

*Mercy Minutes:
  Daily Gems from the Diary of Saint Maria Faustina Kowalska.*
  Fr. George W. Kosicki, CSB. Marian Press

Mother of Mercy Scriptural Rosary.
  Vinny Flynn. MercySong.

The Liturgy of the Hours. 4 Vols.
  Catholic Book Publishing Co.

Spirituality

A Desert Place.
  Adolfo Quezada. Living Flame Press.

Consoling the Heart of Jesus: A Do-it-Yourself Retreat.
  Fr. Michael Gaitley, MIC. Marian Press.

Crossing the Tiber.
  Steve Ray. Ignatius Press.

Extreme Makeover: Women Transformed by Christ,
  Not Conformed to the Culture.
  Teresa Tomeo. Ignatius Press.

Gift and Mystery.
  Pope John Paul II. Doubleday.

God, Father and Creator: A Catechesis on the Creed.
  Pope John Paul II. Pauline Books & Media.

God is Love.
  Encyclical Letter of Pope Benedict XVI.
  Pauline Books & Media.

Live Jesus!: Wisdom from Saint Francis de Sales and
  Jane de Chantel.
  Edited by Louise Perrotta. The Word among us Press.

Mother Teresa of Calcutta: A Personal Portrait.
  Fr. Leo Maasburg. Ignatius Press.

No Turning Back: A Witness to Mercy.
 Fr. Donald Calloway, MIC. Marian Press.

Parenting on Purpose.
 Jason Free. MarcySong/Ignatius.

Rediscover Catholicism.
 Matthew Kelly. Beacon Publishing.

St. Maximilian Kolbe: Martyr of Charity.
 Fr. Peter D. Fehlner, FI. Academy of the Immaculate.

Surrender! The Life Changing Power of Doing God's Will.
 Fr. Larry Richards. Our Sunday Visitor.

Swear to God: The Promise and the Power of the Sacraments.
 Scott Hahn. Doubleday.

The Impact of God.
 Iain Matthew. Hodder & Stoughton
 (available in USA from Scepter Publishers.)

The Joy of Knowing Christ: Meditations on the Gospels.
 Pope Benedict XVI. The Word among us Press.

The Lamb's Supper: The Mass as Heaven on Earth.
 Scott Hahn. Doubleday.

Unbound: A Practical Guide to Deliverance.
 Neal Lozano. Chosen Books.

Books and CDs Available from MercySong
www.mercysong.com

7 Secrets of the Eucharist
Acclaimed by Cardinal George Pell as a "must read," this profound and remarkably readable book by Vinny Flynn will give you a completely new awareness that the Eucharist is not just about receiving Communion; it's about transforming your daily life. Now in its 17th printing, it has remained on the Top Ten Best Sellers list for Ignatius Press since its release in 2007.　　**English Book　$9.95**
Spanish Book　$9.95

7 Secrets Audiobook
A dramatic and inspiring audio presentation of the book, read by the author, with a supporting cast of professional male and female voices and beautiful instrumental excerpts from the *Still Waters* music CD *Benedictus*.　　**2 CDs $16.95**

7 Secrets Study Guide
In this inspiring and easy-to-use guide to her father's book, Mary Flynn leads you on a personal journey to a deeper relationship with Christ in the Eucharist. A great resource for individual use, discussion groups, CCD classes, or RCIA formation.　　**$6.95**

Parenting on Purpose
No dry, philosophical treatise about parenting, this "how-to" book by Jason Free is a straightforward, conversational sharing of specific ways to bring joy to your family and raise your children as real Christians. Often funny, sometimes sad, and always engaging, *Parenting on Purpose* will give you a whole new sense of direction as a parent and help you guide your children (or grandchildren) to a lasting and fulfilling relationship with God.　　**$14.95**

Flynn Family Music

Benedictus
Traditional Holy Hour hymns with new arrangements and an Irish touch. Perfect for Holy Hours, healing services, Adoration, or quiet prayer time. **$15.99**

Endless Mercy
Gentle, healing songs by Vinny Flynn to soothe your spirit or comfort a loved one. Often used for retreats, prayer meetings, and healing services. **$15.99**

Through the Darkness
Erin Flynn's haunting vocals on this award-winning album will touch the depths of your soul, inspiring you to deeper love and trust in God. **$15.99**

Cry Out
John Flynn's collection of original Catholic liturgical songs with a contemporary music style and lyrics that pull the listener into the heart of worship. **$15.99**

Beyond the Veil
Winner of 3 Unity Awards, including "2010 Praise & Worship Album of the Year," this CD by Brian Flynn' presents solid Catholic teaching in beautiful, original songs, featured on EWTN. **$16.99**

We Sing Your Praise II
A collection of inspirational songs from the Flynn family CDs. Includes selections from *Benedictus*, *Cry Out*, *Endless Mercy*, *In the Sight of the Angels*, and *Through the Darkness*. **$15.99**

**Order online at www.mercysong.com
Or call toll free: 888-549-8009**

Devotional CDs

Chaplet of Divine Mercy
The traditional chant version sung by Vinny Flynn & daughters Colleen & Erin, featured for many years on EWTN. Over 80, 000 copies sold.

English CD $15.99
Spanish CD $14.99

The Rosary & The Chaplet of Divine Mercy
Our best-selling CD. Includes recited versions of the Rosary and the Chaplet, with powerful meditations on the Passion from St. Faustina's diary.

$15.99

Mother of Mercy Scriptural Rosary CD Set
"2010 Spoken Word Recording of the Year." This award-winning CD set by Vinny Flynn & Still Waters features a brief scripture reading before each Hail Mary to help you stay focused on the mysteries. Includes all 20 mysteries with beautiful background instrumental music.

2 CDs $17.99

Mother of Mercy Scriptural Rosary Booklet
Pocket-sized booklet with beautiful, original illustrations for each of the 20 mysteries. Perfect for individual or group use, or as a companion to the 2-CD set.

$6.95

The Gospel Rosary of Pope John Paul II
Our most compete rosary set, featuring long & short versions of each of the 20 mysteries. Dramatic readings from scripture, accompanied by beautiful background music, draw you into the Gospel events.

4 CDs $29.99

The Complete Still Waters Rosary
A top seller. The short versions from each CD of the Gospel Rosary, remastered to fit on a single CD. Includes a brief meditation on each of the 20 mysteries.

$15.99

ABOUT THE AUTHOR

Vinny Flynn

Known to many as "the man who sings the Divine Mercy Chaplet on EWTN," this father of seven has been involved in a ministry of mercy for over forty years, using his gifts of teaching, writing, counseling, music, and prayer to help people understand the teachings of the Church and open their hearts to the healing touch of God's love.

As a teacher and counselor for fourteen years, Vinny experienced first-hand how much healing is needed in the world. Feeling called to respond to this need, he began using his gifts in full-time religious ministry. His powerful teachings on Divine Mercy, Mary, the Sacraments, and the Father's love have made him a popular speaker at parish missions, conferences, and retreats.

A former Executive Editor at the Marian Helpers Center and former General Manager of Divine Mercy International, Vinny was actively involved in spreading the message of Divine Mercy, presenting workshops for religious and lay leaders, and writing or editing various Divine Mercy publications, including the official English edition of the Diary of St. Faustina. His personal, straight-forward style of writing makes theological concepts and the teachings of the Church come alive with new meaning and relevancy. Author of 7 *Secrets of the Eucharist*, and co-author of *The Divine Mercy Message and Devotion* and *Now is the Time for Mercy*, Vinny has also published articles in various Catholic periodicals, including *Catholic Digest, Queen, Columbia, Marian Helper*, and *The Friends of Mercy Newsletter*.

Seen frequently at the National Shrine of Divine Mercy in Stockbridge, MA and on Mother Angelica's EWTN cable network,

Vinny's family music ministry, Still Waters, features himself and his daughters Colleen, Erin, and Mary, with support vocals from Vinny's wife Donna and their four sons, John, Tim, Brian, and Kevin. The music is gentle and prayerful, with haunting guitar and violin interludes.

In 1993, Vinny and Donna, with all seven of their children involved in Catholic music and ministry, established a recording/publishing company to produce and distribute their family music CDs, talks on tape, and religious publications.

In 2003, the family ministries were incorporated under the name MercySong, Inc. as a 501c(3) Catholic not-for-profit organization dedicated to bringing healing to others by leading them to a personal experience of the Father's love through music, teaching, writing, counseling, and prayer.

Vinny's book *7 Secrets of the Eucharist* has been acclaimed by Cardinal George Pell as "a must read for Catholics." Published in 2007, the book has remained on the Top 10 Best Sellers list for Ignatius Press. Now in its 17th printing (90,000 copies sold), *7 Secrets of the Eucharist* has been translated into several languages and is also available as an audiobook (2 CDs).

YOUR OWN
NOTES AND PRAYERS

APPROACH THE SACRAMENT OF RECONCILIATION WITH
GREATER LOVE AND FERVOR

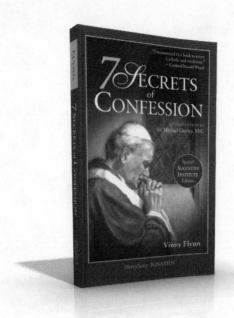

7 SECRETS OF CONFESSION
VINNY FLYNN

Best-selling author Vinny Flynn explores the "hidden" truths of this encounter with Jesus, presenting what to many will be a whole new way of going to Confession, and inviting you to begin an exciting personal journey to healing and holiness. If you do not yet look forward to Confession in the same way you look forward to Communion, this book will change your life.

BROWSE SOME OF OUR MOST POPULAR BOOKS
AND SEE OUR COMPREHENSIVE LIST OF TITLES

AUGUSTINE INSTITUTE

To learn more, visit us at
augustineinstitute.org/books
or call (866) 767-3155

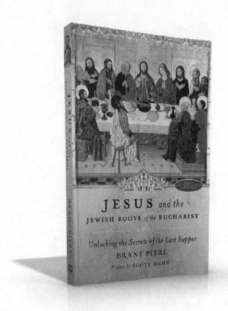